IN THE STORM OF THE EYE

IN THE
STORM
OF EYE
THE

A LIFETIME AT CBS

Bill Leonard

G. P. PUTNAM'S SONS   New York

Joan Sanger and Faith Sale, the editors of this book, have contributed immeasurably to it, and I am profoundly grateful for their help, their patience and their encouragement.

Copyright © 1987 by William A. Leonard
All rights reserved. This book, or parts thereof,
may not be reproduced in any form without permission.
Published by G. P. Putnam's Sons, 200 Madison Avenue,
New York, NY 10016
Published simultaneously in Canada by
General Publishing Co. Limited, Toronto

All photographs courtesy of CBS News
The author gratefully acknowledges permission from Macmillan
Publishing Company to reprint material from *Special: Fred
Freed and the Television Documentary* by David G. Yellin
and Fred Freed. Copyright © 1973 by David G. Yellin and
Fred Freed.

Design by Anne Scatto/Levavi & Levavi
Typeset by Fisher Composition, Inc.
The text of this book is set in Electra.

Library of Congress Cataloging-in-Publication Data

Leonard, Bill, date.
In the storm of the eye.

1. CBS News. 2. Television broadcasting of news—
United States. 3. Leonard, Bill, date.
4. Journalists—United States—Biography. I. Title.
PN4888.T4L43   1987   384.55′4′0973   86-30302
ISBN 0-399-13255-4

PRINTED IN THE UNITED STATES OF AMERICA
1 2 3 4 5 6 7 8 9 10

To Kappy, my beloved wife

CONTENTS

IN THE STORM
OF THE EYE

FOREWORD

There seems no end to books about CBS, but there has not been and won't be one quite like Bill Leonard's. I don't think there was ever anyone in the establishment with his range of experience. From radio and TV street reporter for the local New York station to President of the news division with its enormous and baffling complexity of gadgets and personalities—this is quite a sweep. Rare is the executive who comes from the dangerous side of the camera.

Leonard coped with Dartmouth, the Navy, newspaper city rooms and even advertising agencies before he got into broadcasting and broadcasting got into him. He had a natural understanding of the easily inflated, easily deflated egos whose fate and fortune it was to look that awful machine in its unblinking red eye and utter for the multitudes. He went eyeball to eyeball with the formidable likes of the dictator Trujillo, the tycoon Bill Paley and the boxer Joe Louis (for two very careful rounds).

This book is the inside story of the legendary CBS news operation in what one might call the post-Murrow era. It may be true that during these years television news has become more the producer's and editor's medium than the writer's, and I rather deplore this. In any case, Bill Leonard explores and explains this period, and since he is a born writer himself (no ghosts here, no "as told to"), his book comes off extremely well.

Eric Sevareid

1

EXIT WALTER, ENTER DAN

The deal that kept Dan Rather at CBS and made him anchorman and managing editor of the *CBS Evening News* to the extraordinary tune of $2.2 million a year was struck late on the afternoon of February 7, 1980. Gene Jankowski, head of the CBS Broadcast Group, and I said yes to the last of a long shopping list of his demands, some of them financial, some of them editorial, presented by his agent, Richard Leibner.

The circumstances that had brought us to that point were curious, to say the least. First, that Walter Cronkite's job, unarguably the most secure in America, would be open at all. Second, that Rather, a man of virtually no anchor experience, should be chosen over Roger Mudd, who had substituted for Cronkite for nearly a decade. Third, that a network would be willing to pay more to a comparative rookie than it was paying to the most trusted man in America.

At any rate, there came a moment when Leibner, a man of high surface emotions and sweeping expressions of affection, said, "Baby, I think maybe we've got ourselves a deal."

"Richard," I groaned, "all that means is you've got every damned thing you want. Everything. You haven't left us with a single thing."

"Oh yes I have, baby. I've left you Rather."

One day in July 1978 I was named to be the next President of CBS News, to succeed Richard S. Salant, who had been President of News almost since the Sermon on the Mount and would shortly reach retirement age. He made no bones about it: He would have liked to stay on forever. Salant often said every day in his job was a joy. There are people who enjoy walking barefoot across beds of red-hot coals.

Still, Salant stood by with good grace for more than nine months, a lame duck, watching me make mistakes he would have avoided, and announced he would go to NBC. At the same time he kept singing the praises of CBS News. You couldn't blame him. CBS News was the place of Edward R. Murrow, where Sevareid worked, which Salant himself had helped greatly to build.

And CBS News was, now, above all, the place of Walter Cronkite.

Within forty-eight hours of my return to News from Washington, where I had been a vice president of CBS Inc., Walter was in my office.

In the thirty-odd years that Cronkite and I had worked and played together we had had only one difference. I had been in charge of the coverage of the political conventions in 1964, and, in a particularly silly management move, I had allowed Walter to be temporarily removed from the anchor booth.

Time is the miracle healer. Long before 1978 Walter had forgiven if never forgotten these trespasses. He had gone on to become Mr. Everything, and the *CBS Evening News* had been first in the ratings for so many hundreds of weeks that even the most optimistic dreamers at ABC and NBC News despaired of unseating CBS while Walter still reigned. We had become good friends again, and fate decreed that I should now be what Walter would sometimes refer to as his "boss"—which might be technically true, but he knew, and I knew, that his only boss was his wife, Betsy.

"Bill," said Walter, "I'm absolutely delighted. I don't have to tell you that."

"I like to hear it from you, Walter. I really do. Is there anything I can do for you? Is everything all right?" I meant, If everything isn't all right, if you'd like the East Side moved over west, please let me know, we'll have it arranged by the time you get to work in the morning.

"Well . . . well, Bill, actually, there's one little thing."

"Go right ahead, Walter." Danger. There *are* no little things with Walter Cronkite.

"Well," he said, "I want to give up the *Evening News*."

I didn't say anything.

Walter harrumphed. Cronkite is a world-class harrumpher.

"I mean it," he said. "I told Salant I was thinking seriously about it, but he wouldn't listen. Do you know what kind of a weight it is carrying this thing on your shoulders, week after week, month after month, year after year? You ought to have *some* idea. It's getting to me. I need time. Time to sail. Time to relax. Time to . . . aw, hell . . . it's getting me down. I'd be a damn fool not to quit while I'm ahead."

"Thanks, Walter, I'm glad you came around, I really am." I tried to smile.

Walter said, "Aw, shucks." Walter is one of the few remaining souls alive who actually says, "Aw, shucks," and Betsy would say it makes you want to hug him.

Somehow the old line, How do you handle a 500-pound gorilla? Answer: Very carefully, flashed through my mind.

"Look Walter. Sir. I know you're serious. Let's wait until Dick has gone and then if you still feel this way—which I sincerely hope you won't—maybe we'll have another talk."

"You're a smooth one, Leonard," said Walter, smiling a little, I thought with relief. "You're putting me off."

"Damn right, Walter."

I told Salant about it. "Oh, hell," he said, "Walter does that every hour on the hour. Just roughing up the new boy. Forget it." I forgot it. But Cronkite didn't.

A few months after Salant had gone and I was as much in charge as I would ever be, Walter was back, and this time there was a firmer set to his jaw.

"I want to get it straightened out," he said. "I can't take it much longer. I want to stay with CBS News, do documentaries, make a real contribution, but not be tied down to that day-to-day grind."

Cronkite had a contract that bound him till he was sixty-five (late in 1981), with lucrative retirement provisions beyond that. He was certainly aware that the commercial world outside of CBS was ready to embrace him with gold beyond measure. Walter, like most of us, has a healthy admiration for the American dollar. He is a serious journalist, of course, and to him the best of all beautiful worlds is being paid a hell of a lot for doing what he does best. But maybe not every single day of the week.

When I was convinced that Walter was in deadly earnest and could not be dissuaded, I said something like this to him, over the course of several meetings: "I know what you want in terms of money and security, and I'll try to arrange it. But we want some things, too. First, time to make what you recognize is a very difficult transition. That means doing the *Evening News* for almost another year. Second, cooperating in the transition, which I'm sure you would want to do anyway. Third, remaining part and parcel of CBS News and nowhere else . . . no air work elsewhere unless we give you specific permission." Walter agreed.

Gradually, not without some difficulties, a deal was worked out. To this day Walter remains a part of CBS News as not only a special correspondent but also a director of CBS (although the CBS Board appointment was not a part of his retirement deal). Whether or not he has pangs of regret about leaving the *Evening News* when he did is another question. My strong impression is that Walter, like thousands of others who could hardly wait for the easier life of retirement, soon wished he were back at the old stand.

For the better part of a decade insiders and outsiders had speculated on the question of who might, on some dim dark day, succeed the unsucceedable. Almost like wondering what would happen if God resigned—would it be Allah or Vince Lombardi?

One could hardly exaggerate the importance of the anchor decision. Dollars were riding by the millions, of course. They always are in television. You get used to that. Just add more zeroes.

For generations journalists got their paws on so little money and covered so many rich men who turned out to be crooks that it was easy for them to believe money might be corrupting. In television, with money to the right of them and money to the left of them, the best news people lived in a love-hate relationship with the dollar and its pervasive power. They hated much of what it was doing to the craft they treasured, but they accepted the riches it thrust upon them.

In the grimiest commercial terms, each rating point gained or lost by the CBS Evening News meant millions to the network. And year after year Walter Cronkite came through with a one- or two-rating-point lead over NBC, usually more over ABC. But that wasn't all. Evening News leadership meant—still means—leadership in network news in the public mind, and that translates throughout the day. It helps deliver more viewers into the evening entertainment schedule. Prestige and money. And now the wonderful goose that had been turning out those golden news eggs for so many years would lay no more.

My first important assignment as President of CBS News had ended in failure: trying to persuade Cronkite to stay on. I was not at all confident that I could handle the second: Walter's replacement.

I knew one thing, though. Walter's leaving opened up a tremendous opportunity for the other news divisions, which had languished in the wake of CBS News since the era of Chet Huntley and David Brinkley on NBC. It took Roone Arledge no more time than it takes to say "Monday Night Football" to realize it. For all the efforts ABC had made to get serious about news, no ABC news anchor seemed to have become a real public favorite. No one like the old Huntley-Brinkley team, and certainly no one like Cronkite. But with Cronkite stepping down, Arledge and company thought they might eventually have the answer.

Dan Rather.

Ah! Dan Rather.

I would certainly be stretching the truth if I said I had "discovered" Dan Rather. Ernest Leiser, a perceptive news executive, spotted the young Rather in 1962 covering a flood in his native Texas and brought him to CBS News. Rather was nurtured carefully over the next fifteen years—not because anyone thought of him as a replacement for Cronkite but because we thought he had extraordinary capacity for growth. (Actually, sometimes when we would transfer Rather, trying to develop his career, he became paranoid, suspecting we were somehow trying to thwart it. Perhaps that is in the natural order of things; I had been a correspondent and I'd sometimes suspected the motives of managers.) Early on I saw in Dan a fellow who somehow fit the mold of the Kennedy inaugural speech, a man who would "go anywhere, pay any price." There was something of the hero about him. He was a little foolish, unpolished—this was years ago—but bursting with energy, unafraid, ready to live up to a cliché like "When the going gets tough, the tough get going."

In those early years Rather was self-consciously callow and uneducated, to the extent that sophisticated colleagues snickered behind his back. But he kept coming and learning and asking for more. Gordon Manning, Dick Salant's hard-news deputy, and I recognized Rather's plusses, and experience took care of some of the minuses. Rather was sent to London and learned the ways of a foreign correspondent. He volunteered early and stayed long in dangerous places in Vietnam, while one or two colleagues who looked down on him declined to serve there, including Roger Mudd. He spent three tough years as White House correspondent during the Watergate years, standing up to President Nixon—which many thought he did to a fault, particularly in one quick, bitter exchange that for years had him labeled a liberal in conservative circles. I always found Rather apolitical. I had the feeling he would have made a remarkable soldier, a seeker after glory, ready to risk the hottest fire for a chance at a top rung of history.

By the time Walter Cronkite decided to "retire," Rather was no longer callow. He was seasoned. He was—as he always had been—handsome. He was famous.

And he was the object of desire of ABC and NBC. What about CBS?

The question I faced was simply this: How to structure *CBS Evening News* without Cronkite? There were three options.

Roger Mudd. An unpopular choice in the executive suites at CBS and among our affiliates, circles in which he was unwilling to glad-hand, but probably the odds-on choice among senior news people, particularly those based in Washington. A very good political and election-night reporter. Not much field experience outside of Washington. A superb news reader.

Charles Kuralt. A man who had developed a considerable and deeply devoted following. His "On the Road" pieces on the *Evening News* were perennially engaging. He hosted *Sunday Morning* and had turned that wasteland into something of a television garden. And he was struggling manfully as anchor of the *CBS Morning News*. When he substituted for Walter on the *Evening News* during the "Who'll succeed Cronkite" period in the summer of '79 he seemed so relaxed, comfortable and old-shoe that hundreds wrote urging his selection.

Dan Rather. Clearly up-and-coming. He had most recently blossomed as a correspondent on *60 Minutes*, and the ratings of that program confirmed it. He had shown he was a superb convention-floor reporter and a cool hand in a crisis. As an election-night studio reporter, he seemed to me and others to be perhaps the very best we had ever had, hardly even excepting Walter himself.

There it was. Those were the only choices, really—bearing in mind that *no one* could replace Walter Cronkite.

As for my opinion, the truth is that I had no clear notion of the right way to solve the dilemma of the Cronkite succession. Yes,

Mudd was the smoother broadcaster, yes, Rather was a dynamic personality (I dreaded the mark he might make elsewhere if coaxed away from CBS), and, yes, Kuralt gave people that comfortable, open-hearth feeling.

I did know one thing: Both Mudd and Rather had contracts due for renewal within the next year. It seemed prudent to try to sign them more or less routinely to contract renewals, regardless of whether an anchor assignment for one or both of them might evolve later.

Mudd's contract expired in December 1980; it was early in the year when we talked in my office and I told him I wanted to renew right away, at a very large increase. Formal conversations with Roger are never easy. He is categorically uncomfortable with bosses. As a friend of his once put it, "Roger hates up." At any rate, I remember it as a very short meeting at the end of which Roger said he would let me know whether he would sign right away or let his contract drift on toward its expiration. After a week or two our business affairs officer, Art Sekerak, was told by Mudd's agent that our offer was being turned down. In the months that followed, while the negotiations with Dan Rather swayed back and forth, there never was a word from Roger Mudd, not even a visit from his agent. It always remained a mystery to me why Mudd stayed so aloof from a process that deeply involved his career. Was it pride? Strategy? I never knew then and do not to this day.

In contrast to Mudd, Dan Rather, through his agent, Richard Leibner, expressed open interest in a new contract. His services, it soon became apparent, were on the market. What they were worth depended a good deal on how CBS News solved, or at least tried to solve, the Cronkite succession question, and how Rather was valued by ABC or NBC.

There was some division of opinion among my closest news deputies—Burton (Bud) Benjamin, Ed Fouhy and John Lane. Benjamin favored Mudd from first to last. I knew that Dick Salant would have come down strongly for Mudd, and with him Gordon Manning, with whom I worked for so many years. Fouhy and

Lane were not quite a generation younger, and whether that had anything to do with it or not I don't know, but they voted for Rather.

I talked it over a good deal with Benjamin, the number-two man in the news division. I remember him saying one day, "If it was left to you—and I guess it *is* pretty much left to you—you'd definitely pick Rather, right?"

"No," I said, "only more or less."

"How's that for a definite maybe?" said Bud.

I *did* favor Rather, but with reservations. The anchorperson, far more than the News President, gave CBS News its image. Did Rather have the "character" to fill those shoes? I wondered.

Perhaps there was another solution.

Why not a double anchor? The *CBS Evening News*, with Dan Rather in New York and Roger Mudd in Washington. Double anchors, usually a man and a woman, work well in local television all over the country. But they also have drawbacks, technical and, well, emotional. But not even excepting Cronkite, the most dominant anchor team in television history had been the Huntley-Brinkley combination in its prime in the 1960s. Chet and David dominated not only the evening news but the political conventions and election night as well. Few people, even television news people, remember that there was a period of six or seven years when by most standards of measurement NBC, not CBS, was number one in news.

Looking back at it from the point of view of the weasel-in-charge at the time, it did seem to make a certain amount of sense—perhaps we could plug the gap left by the departure of one *great* man by filling it with two *good* men.

First you have to catch your men.

Rather was sounded out. How would he feel about sharing the anchor spot with Roger Mudd? Rather told us he had nothing but high regard for Roger, and if that's the way management wanted to slice the pineapple it would be all right with him, all other things being equal (all other things being the right contract). This was before the bidding for Dan's services by the other networks got so hot and heavy.

Bud Benjamin and I knew Mudd might be a different proposition. Ever since Harry Reasoner left for ABC, there had been no better correspondent in the shop than Roger Mudd to fill in when Walter was vacationing or away on assignment. Indeed, all the way back in 1964 (more on that later), it was the young Roger Mudd to whom the company turned when Cronkite was temporarily replaced at the Democratic Convention. Therefore, by precedence at the very least, Mudd, his colleagues and the general public had come to accept him as the natural successor to Cronkite.

We also were aware that Dan Rather did not make Roger Mudd's short list of beloved colleagues. Maybe not even his long list.

I suggested that Bud Benjamin, who was closer to Mudd than I, do the asking.

Bud reported later on their lunch in the Edwardian Room of the Plaza Hotel. "I said, 'Roger, how would you feel—just supposing it might happen—how would you feel about doing a coanchor of the *Evening News*, you and Rather?' Mudd didn't even miss a beat. 'I wouldn't do it,' he said. I said, 'That's final?' And he said, 'Yep.' And that was that."

I asked Bud and then John Lane and Ed Fouhy if they thought Mudd's quick turn-off was a ploy to get the anchor job alone or whether he really meant that he wouldn't work with Rather. They all agreed: He meant it.

And so, cut off at the pass, I became firm and decisive. Among the three possibilities, a *single* anchor seemed a reasonably clear choice; I felt there was simply too much of a contrast in personalities to consider Rather and Kuralt together.

I reviewed again in my own mind the qualifications desirable in a network news anchor.

First. He should have excellent journalistic credentials and be an attractive, convincing broadcaster. Simply being attractive is not enough, not at the network-news level, at any rate. "Convincing" has as much to do with what the viewer brings to the screen as the broadcaster. If the viewer has seen the anchorman deeply involved in a variety of news situations in the past, then he or she, as well as the anchorman, brings that experience to the tube. All three—Mudd, Kuralt and Rather—scored well here, although Kuralt had, and still has, a much softer, less "hard-news" image.

Second. He should be at his best in a crisis, quarterbacking a major story. In the so-called good old days of the television news business, the prestige, and indeed the rating, of news divisions rose and fell on performance at the political conventions and election night. Not so much anymore. In today's world of satellite electronics the ability of a news division to act swiftly and surely in a crisis is what counts. And the ability of the top man to perform quickly and confidently, under emergency conditions, is very important. It takes stamina, lots of it, and a zest for working a little harder, somehow doing one's best under the worst conditions. Cronkite was not called "Ironpants" for nothing. There was always a little toilet built near his convention anchor booth. I suppose he must have used it once in a while, but mighty seldom. At any rate, on the "crisis" front it was no contest. Charles Kuralt preferred the quiet country road to the city in turmoil. Roger Mudd, I felt, had neither the stamina nor the competitive appetite to match Rather's.

Third. (This point, not nearly as important, is what one might call the representation factor.) Cronkite was—still is—a marvelous ambassador from CBS and CBS News to the public and indeed to the hundreds of CBS radio and television stations. Walter really enjoyed glad-handing, or when he didn't he took pains to conceal it. Even those who hated CBS News most often loved Cronkite more, because there was something in him that liked them out there. I saw many of these same qualities in Kuralt and only to a slightly lesser degree in Rather. Roger Mudd was quite another story. Essentially he is a very private person.

Thus—enthusiastically backed by Gene Jankowski—I settled on Rather. I never talked with Chairman Bill Paley on the subject, except for one critical and memorable meeting.

But that was really the beginning of the story of the anchor transition, not the end of it. For by the time we had settled on Rather as a first choice, his agent had found out that there was a very high degree of interest in Dan at the other two news networks. Not only was ABC in particular deeply interested in Dan as a potential anchorman, but it was interested in denying Rather to CBS News at a time when Cronkite was bowing out. Whether it was audience research or simply news "feel" that informed them, Arledge and his colleagues felt that Rather would be the strongest possible Cronkite replacement. I never did conduct any audience research on the subject, and I would not have trusted the results if I had. People can compare their reactions to two different anchormen; asking them to evaluate two *potential* anchormen is asking too much. In any case, I soon found myself caught in the middle of a bidding war, involving all three networks, but mostly ABC, which Richard Leibner skillfully exploited.

Rather, closely advised by his wife, Jean, was for many weeks torn between the attractive blandishments of ABC (to say nothing of the prospect of making more than $2 million a year) and the CBS challenge of trying to fill the biggest boots in the news business. If you have been paying a man $300,000 a year, it is not easy to get it through your head that you may have to pay him six times that much, or more, in order to keep him. So I was slow in coming around financially to the point where CBS News had much chance to keep Dan, so rich was the ABC offer.

But in other ways we kept the pressure on. In the months of negotiations just about every "good friend" inside and outside of CBS News was enlisted to call him, visit him, plead with him. But the reports filtering back to me were mostly discouraging. "He's gone," one of my best sources reported sadly early in December 1979. "He's out the window."

"Why?" I asked, incredulous. "I can't understand *why*. Why would anyone want to leave CBS News and a chance to succeed Walter Cronkite?"

"Fear," he said. "Fear and money."

Was Dan Rather *afraid* of the Cronkite challenge? I didn't believe it. He had his faults, but he didn't scare. Money? Well, if we really wanted Dan Rather, it was obvious we would have to pay for it in terms that I was just beginning to comprehend. Incidentally, throughout these negotiations I had only glancing personal contact with Dan himself. When I did see him he was ingratiating, as always. And impossible to read. I had the feeling he did not know himself which way to jump. That meant we had a chance.

Through Art Sekerak and one or two other sources I tried to estimate what kind of money Rather had been offered by ABC, and perhaps by NBC. The figure I kept getting back was more than $2 million a year, plus a big editorial package, whatever that meant. I shuddered. Our best offer to that point had not exceeded $1 million annually. That was the level of authority I had unofficially been granted by Gene Jankowski. Nor had I conceded to Rather the "managing editor" title, which underscored the fact that the anchorman was in fact the boss of the *Evening News* broadcast.

It was not until a late afternoon early in February that I sat down in my office with Richard Leibner and, in the presence of Art Sekerak who might be able to testify later that whereas I might have been insane I had not had a gun to my head, put on the table a package that was as close as I could estimate to what he was being offered elsewhere. And I granted the important point about the title of managing editor of the *CBS Evening News*. My offer was roughly double anything that we had come up with before. As I spelled it all out, I could see Leibner's eyes widen.

"I have to tell you, Bill," he said, "I honestly never expected anything like this."

"Neither did I," I said.

"You can say that again," said Art Sekerak.

"This could be a whole new ball game," said Leibner, after we had massaged those ridiculous figures for half an hour or so.

"That's terrific," I said. "We're all just journalists in this here thing together, huh?"

"C'mon, Bill," Leibner said. "No jokes. I think maybe I can sell this package to Dan and Jean. What about you? Can you handle your side of it across town?"

"If I can't," I said, "I'll be coming to you for a job. If I were Paley I'd throw me out on my ear."

Leibner got up to leave.

"Richard," I said, "you have an honest face."

"What's the hook?" he said, frowning.

"Now that you've had me, I suppose I'll never see you again."

When Leibner had left, I picked up the Exec—the private telephone line connecting about a hundred top CBS executives, making them feel important and leaving the regular phones free for secretaries to gossip with each other. I dialed Gene Jankowski. He left me pretty much alone to run the news division. But the Rather decision, to say nothing of the Rather money, is not something a prudent man would fly blind. Jankowski had followed my long, fumbling trail through the forest of the Cronkite-Mudd-Rather negotiations and basically had been supportive. I hoped we could stick together through the final critical stage.

"Gene," I said, "it really looks like we're going to keep Rather."

"That's terrific. Are you sure?"

"Leibner and I have something just short of a kissing agreement."

"That's great." Pause. "You didn't have to . . . ah . . . sweeten the deal, did you?"

"Gene, there was a little give-and-take on a few minor points."

"What does that mean?"

"Gene, I want you to remember what you said to me when this first got expensive."

"What was that?"

"After it's all over people will forget all about the money."

"I . . . I don't remember saying that."

"Well, whatever." Gene Jankowski is one of the best arguments I know for getting up before dawn and going to early Mass. Every day. Something good must have happened from all of those cold mornings he spent in church. It's hard to find fault with Gene. Still, at the moment of that phone call, and during a chat in his office later in the afternoon, I was faintly uneasy. Was Gene fully aware of what I—and, of course, he—had committed to? He seemed almost casual about this—the culmination of six months of tense negotiations, for most of which time Dan Rather appeared certain to have flown to another network.

"Go over the figures again with me," said Gene.

I went over the figures.

"And you think the back-and-forth is over?"

"You and I are meeting with Leibner at six tomorrow night. In your office, if it's all right."

"Sure it's all right. Why wouldn't it be all right?"

I hesitated. "Gene," I said, "I just wondered whether you were going to run this through Paley."

"I don't know. I'll have to think about that. I'll let you know."

What to tell Paley. What not to tell Paley. Always the nagging question for all senior CBS executives, almost all of whom, sooner or later, drowned in the equally dangerous waters of telling Paley too much or telling him too little. Telling him little was the safest course up to the fatal point where he might read about it in the paper—or see it on TV. Keeping him well posted invited a series of staggering follow-up questions, based on his curious mixture of ignorance and intuition. Questions that could turn a favorite son into a man on the street. For over half a century battalions of shrewd, ambitious and self-confident men thought they had the secret of "handling" William S. Paley. None ever quite did, even including the great Frank Stanton, who once retreated to his own office after a session with Paley and banged his head against the wall in humiliation and frustration.

At the time of this quite critical event—the passing of the baton from Walter Cronkite to Dan Rather—Stanton, having reached sixty-five, had been retired, hoist by his own petard, some said, of rules he had himself devised years earlier. Bill Paley saw no reason, or at least no sufficient reason, for such rules to apply to himself. With Stanton gone, Paley was working—or trying to work—with the third of four corporate presidents he had first found and then found wanting. The first, Charles Ireland, had died suddenly after a few months at CBS. The second, Arthur Taylor, also brought in from "outside," made the mistake of telling one or two of the wrong people that he thought Mr. Paley was on the downhill path of life, so to speak. Paley fired him out of hand. A few years later I was brash enough to ask Mr. Paley (I called him "Bill" to his face but somehow to this day think of him as "Mr. Paley") why he got rid of Arthur Taylor. "He thought he was bigger than the company," said the Chairman.

Succeeding Arthur Taylor was John Backe—a dark, quiet, intense man who came from inside the company, albeit the publishing arm, not what we old-timers regarded as the real company: broadcasting. Backe was nominally Gene Jankowski's boss, just as Paley was *his* (and everyone else's) boss. It was John Backe who had asked me, less than two years earlier, if I would come back from Washington to run CBS News.

I don't know what oracles Jankowski consulted, but he told me we would meet the next morning in the small conference room off his office on the 36th floor of Black Rock, the CBS Building: William S. Paley, John Backe, Gene Jankowski and I.

I asked a friend of mine once to tell me something about his career at IBM. "One long meeting after another," he said.

And indeed, life in business, even the news business, seems to exist only when two or more people are gathered together. Meetings are so commonplace, and so little that is memorable ever takes place in any of them, that company jokes have a tendency to center around stories about meetings at which something actually *did* happen. Will you ever forget the time Caswell fell asleep at the Finance Board meeting, fell off the chair and broke his elbow? A meeting to remember!

In my lifetime of meetings the small gathering to consider Dan Rather's contract stands out above all the rest. Gene and I began by violating a fundamental principle of meeting management: Be prepared. Robert Moses, a wickedly tough executive but a very good one, told me once, "Never call a meeting unless you know exactly what the result is going to be." In this case neither Gene nor I knew what the result would be. Furthermore, in the preceding twenty-four hours, he on his side of town and I over at News on West 57th Street had been so overwhelmingly busy that we hadn't taken the necessary half hour or so to sit down and plan the selling of Dan Rather to John Backe and Bill Paley. And both of these men seemed faintly annoyed at being called into an unscheduled meeting on very short notice. Or was this my own apprehension, reading trouble ahead where none might exist?

"All right, Gene," said the Chairman, "what's this all about? The Rather business, isn't it?"

"Yes, sir," said Gene, smiling. "The news is really good." He looked sideways at me. "Bill has worked very hard, as you know, to keep Dan from leaving. He's very much in demand from both other networks. We've all worked on it. Every one of us."

"I know all that," snapped Paley. "What I can't understand is why in the world would he *want* to leave CBS? Why would it even cross his *mind*?"

"Money," I said.

There was a moment of quiet while that most American of all words—except perhaps "touchdown"—had its full impact.

"What does that mean?" the Chairman growled. "We have money. What's going on here?"

Gene smiled at Bill Paley, the warm smile that so obviously came from his heart. Gene wore optimism like a suit of polished armor. A colleague once said Gene would find something nice to say about a mushroom cloud. "I think it would be a good idea if Bill Leonard brought us up to date," he said. "And believe me it's an interesting story."

If I had been a little smarter, I would, at that moment, have frozen with fear. But I was far too pleased at the accomplishment of keeping Rather to consider that the price of doing so might very well be my own head.

So I began, careful to include John Backe, who had not yet said a word, in a quick recap of the negotiations. "As I think you know, Rather has become an extremely desirable property. All three networks see him—either now or in the immediate future—as the answer to their news anchor problems."

"What made us decide on Dan Rather?" burst out John Backe. "I don't even trust Dan Rather. There's something about him . . ."

I could see a frown forming on Paley's brow. *"They* think Rather is better than Mudd," he said. "They" being Gene and I, and all those others, from whom he could divorce himself later if the decision turned out to be wrong.

"Yes, we do," I said, trying to sound firm, decisive. "Rather and his agent have played a very good game of high-stakes poker. ABC, and Roone Arledge particularly, is willing to pay damn near any kind of money to get him. I think he really has been tempted to go. Not *just* for the money, but also because he wouldn't have to face the challenge of trying to measure up to Cronkite." I just kept talking. "Over the last couple of months it's been back and forth. One day we think we're close to a deal, next day I'm sure he's out the door. He kept saying it isn't the money, and meanwhile the price has kept going up."

"When they say it isn't the money, it's the money," Gene offered in support.

"I don't understand what this is all about, Gene," muttered the Chairman, obviously wishing he were somewhere else. It was late afternoon, and his normal schedule had him back in his lovely Fifth Avenue apartment for a little rest before dressing for dinner. "I thought you told me we might have to pay as much as $1 million a year for Rather—isn't that what you said?—*if* we could hold him? Well, goddamn it . . ." Paley seldom swore. When he did, the words rang out like a jackpot in a row of slot machines.

Gene looked over at me beseechingly.

"Mr. Chairman," I said, reverting to the formality of his most exalted title. "To be brief, I think we *do* have Rather, if you approve. I actually have sort of a handshake deal. But the price turns out to be a good deal more."

"What the hell does that mean, 'a good deal more'?" asked John Backe. I had Paley's full attention now.

"Well, some of the things are important only to us in the news division. I gave him the title of managing editor. I really didn't want to do that, until he earned it, the way Cronkite did."

"Who cares about that?" Backe muttered. "What about the money?"

"The total package on the money is $22 million over ten years."

Backe looked me in the eye. "*You made this deal!*" More a statement than a question. Then he fixed Gene with his glare. "And you were in on it?"

Gene nodded.

"And you think you *have* a deal?"

"Yes," I said. "A handshake deal."

"Then unshake it," said John Backe. "That's the most obscene, indecent, irresponsible thing I have ever come across. You vastly exceeded your authority. Vastly. I'll never okay something like this as long as I'm President of this company. Never."

When no one said a word, not even Paley, he went on.

"Didn't it ever occur to you that you would ruin the salary structure of your whole division?"

"I'm worried about what it will do to salaries. Sure I am," I said.

"Then why would you do it?"

"Because I thought it was more important to have Rather and pay the price than take a chance of not having Rather, particularly if he went to ABC. Losing Cronkite, John, is going to be a serious blow. Getting the right replacement is worth any kind of money."

No sooner were the words "any kind of money" out of my mouth than I knew I had made another of the kind of statement that news division presidents sometimes let slip, remarks that seem to brand them forever as fiscally irresponsible, more concerned with the headline than the bottom line.

Now John Backe was charging full ahead. "This company doesn't have '*any kind of money*.' We have whole divisions that don't make $22 million in ten years. Furthermore, I'll say it again, people are pretty smart. If you put Dan Rather up there, people will see in him the same things I do, that he's just too eager to please, trying to be too much to too many people, all at the same time. Not his own man."

Gene stepped in. "You may be right, John." Which meant he didn't think he *was* right. "But I don't think the average person has that perception. Since Dan joined the 60 *Minutes* team two years ago the ratings have moved up even higher. You have to trace it to Dan."

"And remember that time he talked back to Nixon?" persisted John Backe. "What that means is that if he's your anchorman half the people in the country are going to hate him forever."

"Maybe not quite half, John," I said. "People tend to forget those things."

"Not where Nixon is concerned," Backe snapped in response. "But that's not the point. The point is that there are principles involved here. People don't go around throwing away wild amounts of the company's money, threatening the whole structure of the industry."

I had the feeling that I needed help and needed it fast. Paley hadn't said a word since Backe's outpouring. Now he spoke in a soft reminiscing voice. "You're all too young to remember the Jack Benny deal. Well, maybe *you're* not too young, Bill, but that's when I got Jack Benny and his whole kit and caboodle from NBC to CBS, not too long after the war. It was a huge deal at the time. The biggest. I never thought I'd live to see anything approaching that for one man." My heart leapt. Maybe that meant Paley would go along. Then he said, "It's too much money for any one man. Particularly a newsman."

There seems to be a common belief, going back perhaps to the days when reporters were paid just enough to keep them in gin, that news people would be subject to vast temptations if compensated at the level of their fellow men. Actually, it was a woman, Barbara Walters, first to make $1 million a year, who seems to have underscored that in the age of television nothing could keep a good reporter with a good agent from doing for a million dollars what he or she once did for love.

Gene Jankowski stepped in. He said that he'd been in the negotiations with me right along, that he didn't think it could have been handled any better. Then there began a solid hour of cross-examination of Gene and me by Paley and Backe, some pertinent, some on the order of "Why don't you just go back to Walter Cronkite and tell him he has to stay." Hey, Caesar, about that Rubicon, how about making the trip across *next* year?

It seemed to me I was almost certainly facing the prospect of having to meet Richard Leibner and tell him the deal was off. Backe was no less negative as the minutes dragged on, and Paley seemed torn, until I noticed Jankowski tear off a small piece of memo paper from his pad and write on it "1 point = $5 million." What he meant was that each rating point difference on the *Evening News* meant a bottom line difference of $5 million. While Backe and I were arguing, he slipped the little scrap to where Paley could not miss seeing it. Paley read it and looked over at Jankowski. "Is that really true, Gene?" he said.

"Absolutely, Mr. Chairman."

Gene and I exchanged glances. It was time to strike.

"Gentlemen," I said, "we have a meeting with Rather's agent in less than an hour. Do I get a vote of confidence or what?" No one said anything. I tried, foolishly, to make a little joke. "I mean, if this is a democracy"—I didn't even snicker—"I guess you know how I vote."

Gene Jankowski jumped right into the fray. "Naturally, I'm with Bill. We go with the Rather contract."

John Backe was dignified and subdued. "We'd be making a big mistake. I'm still dead set against it."

All three of us looked at Mr. Paley. I thought of the old story of Lincoln's cabinet: Fourteen votes nay, one vote aye; the ayes have it.

Paley spoke slowly and deliberately. "It's been my experience in life," he said, "that some of the cheapest things turn out to be the most expensive and some of the most expensive things turn out, in the long run, to be the cheapest."

He stopped, got up, said thank you, and left.

And Dan Rather became the anchorman of the CBS *Evening News*.

The Rather deal was not formally wrapped up until the morning of February 18, 1980, when his contract was signed. I had had no communication at all from Roger Mudd for many weeks, but the first thing I did after scheduling a press conference in New York was to call him to say I wanted to see him right away. He agreed to meet me later that morning in the CBS News Washington office. I asked Gene Jankowski if I could borrow one of the two company planes, and inside of an hour I was on my way, the only passenger on the deluxe Gulfstream jet.

The meeting was short and ugly. I have no idea whether the news that Dan would succeed Walter came as a surprise to Roger. I find it hard to imagine that he had no inkling of what might be coming.

At any rate, he took it very hard. I told him I had let him know as quickly as I possibly could, but he said it had been handled in a manner that was extremely embarrassing to him and his family, who apparently had heard the news on the radio just before I arrived. His face was pale and his lips bitter and thin, and he asked me if he could be relieved of his contract, which had the best part of the election year left to run. I said, as I recall, that I didn't think so. And I stuck to that. I am very competitive. I did not want Roger Mudd, a first-rate—perhaps the best—network political reporter working for the opposition during a presidential campaign. I told Roger I was sorry I hadn't been able to keep him posted about Rather, but the simple truth was I hadn't known until a few hours earlier whether Dan was certain to stay with CBS. I don't think Roger cared or was even listening to me. He was deeply hurt and felt publicly humiliated. I told Roger that I hoped he would stay with CBS News forever, and I meant it. But I knew in my heart that the price of keeping Dan Rather was even higher than the $22 million: It would include the loss of Roger Mudd.

2

BITTEN
BY THE CBS BUG

W hen I was a small boy I fell in love with radio.

At about the same time that the young Hemingway was embracing Paris, I was wide-eyed over the phenomenon of radio in Orange, New Jersey. My family had a Freed-Eismann set, the latest thing in the mid-twenties. It had three big, black Bakelite dials for tuning and derived its power from an automobile storage battery, half-hidden under a table in our living room. Voices and music from space. How could it be? From way out there. From Pittsburgh. Chicago. On good nights, Denver. My God, even Los Angeles!

Our local paper, the *Newark Evening News*, capitalized on the early radio craze by running what it called a DX column—news and gossip about the kind of rare and distant radio stations one could hear very late, long past bedtime. "William, what are you doing up at this hour?"

My friend Warren Loughlin, who lived up the street, and I began to make lists of the stations we heard. I can still remember the sharp thrill of that forbidden listening, earphones clamped tight, straining to catch the voice of an announcer saying—yes, he did say it— "KFI, Los Angeles."

Warren and I were not only bitten by the DX bug but also captivated by the music that poured out of our sets as radio became more and more a part of everyone's lives. Long before there was a *Lucky Strike Hit Parade*, we would tune in station after station, keeping track of what songs were played most often. We kept lists that went on for pages, and we'd root for our favorites to lead our own personally constructed charts—"Star Dust" and "Time on My Hands" came along just as we got too old for such nonsense.

Somewhere along this electronic road I became interested enough in the technical end of radio to get a ham ticket, and, although I have almost no technical aptitude, I have never lost interest in amateur radio. Hams tend to be a shy lot, enjoying the protection of the distance that both keeps them apart and binds them together. And, as an old-time ham on the third scotch will sometimes confess to another, "After all these years, I still think radio's a miracle."

Somewhere along the way of listening, perhaps in the very early thirties, I became conscious of the difference between radio networks. NBC was strong and showy and rich . . . hell, it had *two* networks, Red and Blue (later the Blue evolved into ABC). What gave me the impression that CBS, although smaller, was somehow more progressive, a little classier, I just do not know. This was long before the Ed Murrow days, but it became fixed in my mind very early on that radio might be my career and CBS the place to work.

Edward Klauber, who became Executive Vice President of CBS a year or so before I went to college, was a friend of my family's. We were living in Westport, Connecticut, then, and he and his wife came up for an occasional weekend. He was a tough, uncompromising man, who had earlier been a night city editor of *The New York Times*. I asked Klauber if he could arrange for me to visit CBS headquarters, then at 485 Madison Avenue. He asked me why I would want to do something like that. I said I loved radio and I hoped someday I might work in radio and I had always felt CBS was the best place of all. "William," he snapped—and I mean snapped: I can remember his snap echoing down through the years—"I will be glad to arrange a tour of CBS for you." Pause. "At the same time I think you should know that you will never work at CBS." Pause. "Before you break into tears, you should know that I have an unbreakable rule that no member or friend of my family ever has worked or ever will work there."

Long before it came to anything like that, Ed Klauber was gone from CBS, a victim of dual problems—health and William S. Paley. But he left an extraordinary legacy. Bill Paley himself once told me that it was Klauber who "educated" him in the news business, in its importance for CBS and in the kind of standards CBS should have, and it was Klauber who encouraged the legendary Paul White, who built the CBS News organization in the thirties and early forties. If Klauber can be considered the father of CBS News, then perhaps it owes its birth to an odd set of circumstances.

The story goes that when Klauber, newly married, was working long, late hours at the *Times*, his wife complained to a friend, the famous publicist Edward L. Bernays, that their marriage wasn't likely to work out. He worked all night and she worked days; they weren't seeing much of each other. Couldn't Bernays find Ed some other job? Bernays was a consultant to Paley and arranged an interview. It wasn't long before Klauber had a job at CBS. In what seemed like no time at all the Klauber marriage was on track. Before too long Klauber was the number-two man at the company, where, among other forthright moves, he fired Bernays.

I knew none of this, of course, when my "tour" was arranged. I remember one moment of it, and one only. At a certain point my guide said, "Now we're going to go into the announcer's booth. You must be absolutely quiet." I felt like asking if it was all right for my heart to beat. "You watch the big clock there and see what happens when the clock hits exactly twenty-nine twenty." At the appointed second the announcer, who earlier had delicately cupped his right hand to his ear, stepped to the mike and said, in tones of infinite depth and richness, "This is CBS, the Columbia Broadcasting System."

It would be gross understatement to report that chills ran up and down my spine. If the time ever came when I might utter those words . . . Ah, bliss. Ah, glory. Imagine. "This is CBS, the Columbia Broadcasting System."

Immature, erratic, unpopular but energetic, I went to Dartmouth College during the Depression years. When it turned out I wasn't nearly as good a football player as I assumed myself to be, I went out for *The Dartmouth*, which in those days was an excellent college newspaper. Budd Schulberg was editor. Eventually I became managing editor. The simple lessons of newspapering I learned in college stood me in very good stead over the years. When it came time to make a living with the rest of the class of 1937, newspapering was one of the few things for which I had any qualifications or desire.

Another was acting. I was never swept away by the theater or theater people, but I enjoyed being in plays. Dartmouth was blessed with a superb drama department headed by a little man by the name of Warner Bentley. I played very solid, sometimes starring roles in a great many productions. As I thought about a career, I wondered about acting. I talked it over with my mother, whose encouragement consisted of her saying to me, "William, I haven't the faintest idea whether you're good enough, but I do know you're not tall enough or handsome enough."

Years later I compared notes with Ed Murrow, and he told me how he too had done a great deal of acting in college and had been encouraged to take it up as a career. God knows with that voice and those looks he might have gone on to the same heights on Broadway or in Hollywood that he achieved in broadcasting. The truth is there has to be a bit of an actor in an anchorman. Serious news people don't like to admit it, but it's true.

There is something of the performer, obviously, in Walter Cronkite. And in fact at one time he was a play-by-play announcer. Mike Wallace did commercials for years and played the lead in a Broadway show. The ranks of NBC and ABC are studded with the names of men and women who have become serious, dedicated newspersons but who somewhere along the line embraced something less than "pure" news.

A succession of men set and maintained the standards that kept CBS News from being swallowed into the trough of commercialism, where radio and television mostly live. Paul White, Frank Stanton, Richard Salant. I think they all feared, as do I, that the enormous drive for dollars always threatens to overwhelm the journalistic integrity of the broadcast news business, as it has done in sports. It is simply an ironic little sidebar that some of our most fiercely independent television journalists have a touch of show biz in their backgrounds. After all, so does the President of the United States.

The year I graduated from Dartmouth, 1937, was the height of the second wave of the Depression. It was not the best time to be starting a career. I gave up the idea of the theater and thought I might try newspapering.

But I hadn't gotten CBS out of my system. Somehow I heard that CBS had developed a training program for college graduates. Each year they would pick six people (men, of course) from the Ivy League (mostly) and rotate them through the company, hoping that, down the line, one or more might flower into a Great Executive. I remembered the announcer's booth and the CBS announcer with his hand cupped behind his ear. Ed Klauber was gone by then, but I had a feeling I was *destined* for CBS. It seemed to me that CBS would be missing a great bet if they passed up a young man who . . .

A month or so after my application went in, I received a letter from a man named Burgess, the CBS personnel director, who explained that there had been more than five hundred applicants for the six spots. They had narrowed down the field to thirty young men who would be personally screened by CBS executives. CBS was obviously showing the kind of common sense one would expect from a company I had selected as the working place of choice. I was in, wasn't I?

One hot day in April 1937 I hitchhiked down from Hanover,

New Hampshire, to New York; the next day I saw several CBS people; the only one whose name I can recall now was a "middle-aged" man named Frank Stanton. He must have been nearly thirty.

A couple of weeks later a letter came from Mr. Burgess saying that the task of selection was proving exceptionally difficult. They had narrowed the thirty down to a final ten. I was one of the ten. They would let me know.

Now I was *really* home.

About a month later I got a final letter from Mr. Burgess saying how dreadfully sorry he was. The choice was almost too difficult to make. But we regret to inform you . . . I sat down and wrote a letter. "You sons of bitches, you've wasted six months of my life. I'll get even with you for this." After an hour or so I tore the letter up and vowed to work there someday.

I did finally catch on at CBS some eight years later. Meanwhile, I spent three years as a small-town newspaper reporter, a couple of years in the radio research department of Newell-Emmett, a New York advertising agency, and four years in the U.S. Navy, where my radio background landed me in the middle of a push-button electronic war within a war that was many dreadful years ahead of its day.

The Germans—under Wernher Von Braun at Peenemünde—developed several types of radio-guided bombs, the most deadly of which was the HS293, a tiny pilotless aircraft containing a single 500-kilogram bomb. These guided missiles were slung under the wings of a Heinkel bomber, inside which a bombardier would visually guide the missile toward its objective, controlling its flight by radio.

A way had to be found to discover what frequencies were being used, and then, if possible, to throw the bombs off target with special jamming equipment. Two small destroyer escorts were loaded with electronic listening equipment and sent to the convoy lanes where the glider bombs were most often used. I had never been to sea nor had I been in combat before, but I found myself in charge of a special unit aboard two ships, the *Herbert C. Jones* and the *Frederick Davis*. Our orders were to get into the middle of a few attacks and see what we could find out.

In Algiers the British told us where we might rendezvous with what convoy and at what precise hour we would be hit by Luftwaffe planes flying out of Marseilles. The Germans arrived on the minute, and the air was presently alive with guided missiles. By a lucky accident, a radio in our communications room had been inadvertently left tuned to a particular channel. That just happened to be one of the frequencies the Germans used to control the missiles. In the next attack, a few afternoons later, we were able to make a recording of their missile control. I was flown to Washington with the precious record, and, on the basis of its information, we began to develop jamming equipment. The jammers were quite successful, and within a few months a fleet of small ships equipped with jammers went along with all our convoys, and with the fleets invading Normandy and southern France. The *Herbert C. Jones* survived the war; the *Davis* was lost in action.

When the war ended I found myself in New York, a lieutenant commander with enough service to earn a quick discharge. I had often thought that if I could survive the war and get back to my "career," whatever that was, by the time I was thirty . . . well, a man couldn't ask for more. I made it with six months to spare.

I went around to the Newell-Emmett agency, where, to my astonishment, I was offered $100 a week to do the same job I had done four years earlier. I asked my old boss, Gerald Tasker, why he was willing to pay me so much—not that I minded. But I told him that the itch I'd had for all these years to work for CBS had not gone away. Would he mind if I tried my hand there, and if that didn't work perhaps I'd come back to Newell-Emmett? Jerry Tasker knew all about my radio ambitions. "I'll even try to get you an appointment over there," he said with a smile.

"With whom?"

"If I can swing it, with Frank Stanton." Tasker and Stanton came from similar backgrounds—radio audience testing—and Jerry was able to arrange an appointment with the man who had, by 1945, become CBS's Executive Vice President and General Manager.

I walked into Stanton's office still in uniform, with the two rows of ribbons to which I was entitled, most of them for simply surviving, arranged across my chest.

"Well, young man," Stanton said, "I see you survived the war in good order. Are you still in the Navy or out?"

"I'm on terminal leave. I can still wear the uniform. I could wear a suit . . . it's just that I . . . I . . ."

Stanton got me off the hook with a smile that he has surely long forgotten but I never shall. "I understand," he said. "If I were you I would do exactly the same thing."

We chatted about "my war" for a few minutes and then, quite abruptly but softly, he asked me what I would like to do at CBS.

I had thought this one over in advance. "My first choice," I said, "would be to be your assistant." I didn't even have the sense to say *one* of your assistants.

"I don't have an assistant," said Frank Stanton. He was probably tempted to say, "and if I had one he certainly wouldn't be you." Instead he asked politely, "Well, what else do you have in mind?"

"Sir," I said, "I've given this a lot of thought. I'd like to be in television."

Stanton's very blue eyes opened wide. He threw back his head and gave what sounded very much like a guffaw. "Bill," he said, "I didn't mean to laugh at you. But do you know how many people we have in this whole company working in television?"

"No, sir."

"Four."

"Four?"

"Yes. If we were to hire you in television it would mean increasing our television personnel by twenty-five percent."

"Well, sir, I didn't mean you to do anything like that."

"I know. You think television is a big part of the future. That's what you meant, isn't it?"

"Yes, sir. That's what I meant."

"Maybe, maybe someday. The man who runs television is a fellow named Larry Lowman. You can go see him."

"Thank you."

"He's one of the nicest men you'll ever meet. But he won't have a job for you. Then I want you to go down to the ninth floor and see a man named Arthur Hull Hayes. He runs WABC. I suppose you know that's our local CBS station in New York."

Frank Stanton then picked up a phone on his desk, dialed a number and said in the quiet, efficient voice that I would get to know so well, "Art, I am sending down a young man named Leonard. He's just getting out of the Navy."

Stanton hung up without small talk, got up from behind his desk and shook my hand. "I hope you land something here," he said.

I went down to the 9th floor and was ushered into a somewhat smaller office occupied by a much larger man, a straightforward radio professional who seemed downright suspicious after I had given him a summary of my experience.

"Mr. Leonard," he said sternly, with the hint of a brogue, "you wouldn't be kidding me now, would you?"

I must have looked as blank as I felt.

"This isn't something you and Stanton cooked up, is it?"

Whatever was going on here was sailing right over my head.

"You told me you were born in New York?"

"Yes, sir."

"And you know the city?"

"Pretty well."

"And you've been a reporter?"

I nodded.

"And done some broadcasting?"

Ever since college I had managed some part-time announcing on Connecticut radio stations, and actually formed a little radio production company, which gave me more experience on paper than I had in reality.

"You may be just the fellow we've been looking for," said Arthur

Hull Hayes. "If it wasn't a joke, I guess I know what Frank Stanton had in mind."

"Exactly what?" I think I said.

"Bill," he said (I was Bill now), "what would you think about doing a radio program for us, twice a day, six times a week, about the city of New York? Think you could handle it?"

I sat silent for a moment, stunned. "Mr. Hayes," I finally managed to say, "what is it you might want me to do on the radio program?"

"Why, we'd want you to be the *host*. The *star*. The man *up front*. You'd have a *staff*, of course."

He couldn't be serious. Big-time radio couldn't possibly work this way.

Suddenly Hayes began selling *me*. "Look, with the war over, we think folks are going to turn back to what's interesting in their hometown. And New York is the biggest, most fascinating town in the country—heck, the world. We want someone who can go out at night, get the feel and smell of the city and report on it first thing in the morning, then come back late in the day and do it all over again. Tough job. We've tried newspaper reporters, even Meyer Berger. They all sound awful. We've tried announcers. They sound like . . . announcers. You might be what we're looking for. I think Frank must have seen something in you, and so do I. Would you like to audition for the job?"

Hayes turned me over to an owlish string bean of a man named Gordon Graham, the program director. Like everyone else at WABC (later to become WCBS), he had only a hazy idea of what the new program would actually be like. "It should have the feel of the city," he said. "The way I see it, you will wander around from about eight P.M. till four in the morning gathering material. Then come in and put it together. Go on the air at six to six-thirty A.M. Grab a little sleep. Go out again and come back in time for the afternoon show. On Saturdays you won't have to do but one show."

I knew the idea was as absurd as the schedule, but the opportunities were unlimited. I did the first of several auditions a couple of nights later, wandering more or less aimlessly around Broadway and Greenwich Village, talking to cops and people in bars and rediscovering New York.

The control room engineer told me years later that my audition was the worst single performance he had ever heard in a radio studio. But, for whatever reasons, I was hired as host of *This Is New York*, which went on the air the morning of December 31, 1945, at an hour when—thank God—there were few awake to hear it. It lasted for seventeen years, and I was its host for thirteen.

Arthur Hayes was right, the town was ready for a program about itself, as young men and women returned to taste the fruits of the great city.

And I was finally at CBS, after those many years of dreaming about it.

Life has funny bounces. Before I walked into Art Hayes's office I had not seriously entertained the idea of an on-the-air career. Twenty years later, I was just as surprised to find myself on the path of management.

3

THE
GOOD OLD DAYS
OF RADIO

S omehow I had been handed the keys to the city. A full hour a day of precious radio time could hardly have been delivered to a more irreverent—but, I must say, energetic—crew than the staff of *This Is New York*. I was the on-the-air man, but by no means the most talented. Most of us were fresh out of service. Our attitude, sometimes expressed openly to our bosses, was cocky, to say the least: "You can fire us but you can't shoot us." We had come from places where the enemy, and indeed our commanders, held our lives in their hands. We were not about to take lip from anyone now.

This Is New York, particularly in its early years, was raw and self-indulgent, but all of the people involved, including some of our bosses, cared very much about writing. Good writing was not in generous supply on radio then, even less than it is on television today. We wrote for ourselves and for each other, paying scant attention to our listeners.

New York: We loved the town, hated the town, laughed at it, did our best to uncover what was sad and what was wonderful about it.

I was a broadcasting amateur, if there ever was one, buoyed by the talents of four young men in particular: Al Morgan, Fred Freed, Martin Weldon and Jim Yankauer. Morgan was a gifted writer, who went on to create a fine novel called *The Great Man* and to produce the *Today* show. He was funny and fast at the typewriter. A page dripping with venomous wit would spew from his machine in three minutes flat. Years later my friend Gordon Manning said about Dick Salant's memos, "He writes 'em faster than I can read 'em." Morgan wrote even faster than Salant could dictate.

Perhaps the deepest talent working with me was a shy young man named Fred Freed. He had been a writer for *Esquire*, and he was a craftsman of the written word. He wrote in the short, spare sentences that were ideal for radio and, in later years, for television. He became one of the greatest television documentary producers. Unfortunately Freed died at a far too early age.

Commercials were something we disliked and were juvenile enough to sneer at openly on the air. No institution was too hallowed to escape the sting of my tongue (my tongue, *our* writing).

But in 1946 radio was the second largest advertising medium in the world. Newspapers came first, but everything else was after radio—magazines, billboards and somewhere down the list skywriting. Television was still around the corner—although it took no genius to sense that the corner was about to be turned.

Still, ratings called the tune then as they do now, and as they will a decade from now. After *This Is New York* had been on the air for two or three months, I was called into the office of the station manager, a tough, colorful man named Richard Swift.

"First," he intoned sternly, "you and those other nuts have got to stop running a gambling hell in your offices."

"It's not a hell," I shot back. "Who would say something like that?" But of course, I didn't deny the charge. We had a lot of interesting games going on in that crazy office of ours.

"One of the secretaries on the floor. She said she felt corrupted.

She says she hears the rattle of dice over the sound of her typewriter."

"A girl like that is sick."

He ignored the remark.

"Don't you guys do any *work*?" he asked angrily.

"Goddamnit, Dick, we work *all night*!" Now I was getting angry.

"That's what I really wanted to talk to you about. Your program
may not be working out."

I had been on the air for about three months, leading into the
Arthur Godfrey show first thing in the morning and into a program
called *The Missus Goes a-Shopping* in midafternoon.

Swift dropped his bomb. "Your numbers don't seem to be adding
up."

"You mean the ratings," I said hesitantly.

"That's right."

"Ratings aren't everything," I tried.

"Name something else," said Swift.

I knew if I offered a pretentious suggestion like "quality" Swift
would throw me out of the office. Instead, I said, "What do you
want me to do?"

"Bill," he said, as if pronouncing a sentence of death, "we are
about to give your show the Stanton-Lazarfeld test."

I thought of some sassy thing to say about tests, beginning with
Wassermann, but the "Stanton" kept me quiet.

"When Frank Stanton was doing audience research years ago, he
and a guy named Lazarfeld figured out this nutty way—well, maybe
not so nutty way—to get people's real reactions to shows. You get a
bunch of jokers off the street, maybe thirty or forty, and you put
them all in a room. You give each person a button in each hand and
you tell them, 'Now we're going to play you this program and when
you hear something you like press the right button, and when you
hear something you don't like press the left button, and then if you
don't feel anything one way or another don't press any button.' Got
it so far?"

I nodded.

"Well, they have all these buttons sort of wired together and the results are plotted against time, from the start of the program to the end, so that what you come out with is a great big chart with this group's reaction to the show, literally minute by minute. The midpoint of the chart is zero, meaning sort of no reactions, but you can look and see if maybe at some particular minute one thing on the show had a very positive or maybe a very negative reaction. You see the beauty of it?"

"It makes me nervous," I said. But what choice did I have?

A few days later Swift called Al Morgan and me into his office to hear the results of the Stanton-Lazarfeld test.

"You're going to be surprised," he said.

That's what I was afraid of.

He had a very large piece of graph paper spread out on his desk. "Take a look at this chart," he said, pointing. "Now, see, this is where the program starts, and you'll notice it goes right away into the red."

"It seems to *stay* there," I said, dismally, noting the line sadly negative, minute after minute.

"Yep. That's the first half of the show, and you haven't hit 'em where they live yet, William."

My eyes moved on across the chart. Suddenly I spotted a brisk positive upturn, a sudden spurt—for about a minute—into the black. "There," I shouted. "Look at that! Whatever I was doing then, they loved it. People *loved* it! You've probably got the script for that day you made the test. What was I doing then? I can do more of that!"

"It was just one minute," said Dick Swift. "And I'm afraid it won't help."

"Why? Why not?"

"Because that was the Chiquita banana commercial."

Al Morgan piped up just then. "It's easy," he said brightly. "We'll play the Chiquita banana commercial for a half hour in the morning and a half hour in the afternoon, they'll love us."

"Shut up, Al," I said. "Can't you see we're being fired? Dick, are we being fired?"

"I think so," he said. "But I'm not absolutely sure."

As it turned out, *This Is New York* was saved, but not by its own virtues. A quirk of scheduling that involved the station's great morning star, the talented and lascivious man in the office next to mine named Arthur Godfrey, somehow put him on earlier in the morning, in one of the spots I had occupied, and opened up three-quarters of an hour for me at 9:00 A.M. My program was restructured to give it a somewhat softer focus, with at least one celebrity interview each day. We were now competing for the visiting Hollywood stars with Dorothy and Dick, Tex and Jinx, Mary Margaret McBride and other hard-hitters of the era. Our taste in guests was eclectic—not all Hollywood by any means. There were people like Robert Moses, Frank Lloyd Wright, Harry S Truman, John F. Kennedy, and, perhaps my own favorite, a person utterly without pretension who appeared four or five times over the years, Eleanor Roosevelt.

On one occasion Mrs. Roosevelt had arrived at the wrong floor, five stories below our studio. Realizing the error, she had tried but been unable to catch an up elevator and had taken the stairs instead, arriving a little late. When she caught her breath, she began apologizing profusely to me. "You must have been worried. I'm terribly, terribly sorry," she said. She was that kind of woman.

Audience reaction, so dismally recorded by that Stanton-Lazarfeld test, turned around smartly soon after our move to the mid-morning hour and the format changes. Ratings improved dramatically, and over the years the show more than held its own opposite Tex and Jinx on NBC, our main competition.

In addition to interviews, we developed a series of continuing features that proved popular. We liked movies and, without taking any surveys, decided our audience would appreciate some straight-from-the-shoulder reviews. Our reviews turned out to be frank, and then some; they were often rough, sometimes downright mean. Such sounds had hardly ever come out of a loudspeaker. Movie companies complained to CBS management, particularly when they were paying to advertise the picture somewhere on the station, but management never let us down. Nowadays, just about every big

New York station has a program that takes a stab at reviewing movies. Back when we did it, the shock effect helped spread the word about *This Is New York* and generated new listeners.

I don't think we were under any illusion that the folks out there all went to the theater, but Broadway had far greater prominence in the late forties and fifties than it has today. Well over a hundred new shows opened each season, sometimes as many as three or four a night. All of us at the radio show were theater buffs, and we decided there was nothing to stop us from reviewing plays as well as motion pictures. So we did. One after another, year after year. I remember the thrilling opening nights of *Death of a Salesman*, *Streetcar*, *South Pacific* and many others. But for every gem I'm still trying to forget scores of horrors. My play critiques were as uncompromising, and sometimes as savage, as the movie criticisms, and this occasionally led to uncomfortable moments. For example, advance scheduling for the program sometimes had stars or playwrights booked before my review was aired. My guest might come marching to the studio ready for a fight. And I would quickly say, "I'll forget it, if you'll forget it," before we went on the air. I had panned a minor play of Tennessee Williams's. He showed up as a scheduled guest a day or two after the opening and answered all my questions by simply saying "yes" or "no," and meanwhile drained a full tumbler of scotch during the interview. It was a tough ten minutes.

Another popular feature on the program was a weekly restaurant review, in which, to avoid any hint of commercialism, I never gave the name of the restaurant. People who wanted the name would have to write or call in; we got hundreds, sometimes thousands, of requests. Our "trick," if you want to call it that, was never to talk about expensive restuarants, but to limit ourselves usually to restaurants where the cost of the entire meal was less than $1.50, almost never more than $2.00! That gave us plenty of eating latitude in those days. New York in the fifties had hundreds of excellent ethnic restaurants where you could gorge for about a dollar, including a fine French place on Ninth Avenue called The Brittany and a marvelous little Chinese basement joint I discovered on Doyers

Street called Wah Kee, where one could eat forever for 80 cents. The proprietor of Wah Kee, Louis Toy, hardly knew what hit him when a mob descended on his tiny place the day after the broadcast about it. He was so grateful, he said, that he wanted to do something for me. I said I would like to know something about Chinese cooking and am now reasonably handy around a wok.

Somehow, in the course of those years at WCBS, I must have learned something: how to broadcast, how to edit radio tape, how to interview. A little here and there.

And how to stay alive in New York City streets at night—which was far easier than it might be today. If I was wandering alone down near police headquarters late at night, I would keep to the center of the street. Probably a dumb idea, but I was never mugged, nor was anyone on the staff. Fred Freed and I particularly loved the cops-and-robbers side of New York life, as we got to know police in many precincts and followed the cops on raids, tape recorders in hand.

The drug scene in those days did not amount to much by today's light. But there was a drug problem and there were drug addicts. *This Is New York* had a serious documentary side to it—perhaps a quarter of its content—and as early as 1950 we did a long series on the life story of a heroin addict, "Robert Adams." All the horror was laid out on audiotape, and it was not much different from an addict's story of today, except that "Adams" was older and his story more shocking because so few had been exposed to it at that time.

When World War II ended there was no practical way to record audio in the field. Although the wire recorder had been invented, it was a fragile device. I can remember doing a radio remote in 1946 from the battleship *Missouri* with the sound transcribed on the spot on huge audio discs. In 1949 Minnesota Mining developed the radio tape recorder for practical commercial use, the most important technological step in radio in a generation. Shortly we were able to buy, and learned to use effectively, portable battery-operated tape machines. The first ones weighed ten times as much as today's equipment. But they worked. A CBS engineer named Joel Tall developed a device that made it comparatively easy to edit the tape.

What we at CBS and other young producers and editors at NBC learned about editing audiotape became the basis for our later expertise in handling film and videotape.

A variation on the bromide that a man is known by the company he keeps is that a company is known by the restaurants it keeps. As with the friends in a man's life, proximity is a governing factor. Before CBS moved to its own building two blocks to the west in 1963, the company rented space at 485 Madison Avenue, on the southeast corner of 52nd Street, taking over more and more floors as it expanded, until just about the only foreigners left were a custom tailor shop specializing in military uniforms, a Spanish tourist office and a dealer in rare jade. In one sense CBS had also taken over the ground-floor restaurant called Colbee's.

Colbee's catered almost entirely to CBS people plus a few who came to meet or stare at CBS people. No sane outsider ever went there twice with the thought of enjoying its food. CBS alcoholics avoided Colbee's because its long bar was conspicuous from an entrance off the Madison Avenue lobby. No one formally lunched or took a guest to Colbee's, but it was always packed at mealtimes with friends and fellow workers. It was so much a part of CBS that there was even a company phone in one corner, as I recall, and if a person was missing from his office area the first call that went out was always to Colbee's. Colbee's didn't deserve the sobriquet of restaurant. It was simply a *place*. Expense-account business lunches most often were held around the corner at Louis and Armand's; "21" was not then, and is not now, far away, for those few at the very top, but Louis and Armand's was a first-rate place to eat and to be seen with clients.

A splendid, soft-spoken agent named Jap Gude, whose clients included Walter Cronkite and who helped Fred Friendly get his first New York job, ate there every weekday for twenty-five years. CBS News people were generally too poor and too pressed for time to enjoy the fruits of places like Louis and Armand's. Ed Murrow more often than not was satisfied with a sandwich and a drink at Colbee's bar. Murrow was as nervous before going on the air as he was cool and controlled once the broadcast had started. He would down his routine shot of whiskey, and it was not unusual for beads of sweat to break out on his forehead. His hands might shake just a trifle. "That's it, brother Bill," he would say, giving me a shy, crooked smile and moving toward the studio. In a few minutes the great organ of his voice would do its work.

Years later Ed told me—and, I suppose, others—that he wished television had never been invented. "Friendly dragged me kicking and screaming into this," he would say, only half meaning it. But he loved radio, and he was marvelously equipped for it. He was like a fine church, offering something to think about and something splendid to listen to.

Ed Murrow to the contrary notwithstanding, in my early New York radio days I had mixed emotions about CBS News, of which I was not then a part. On the one hand, I was coming to know very well and to admire the top correspondents, some of whom appeared as occasional guests on my program—Murrow, Charles Colling- wood, Douglas Edwards, Dallas Townsend, David Schoenbrun, Bob Trout and others. On the other hand, I had a very low opinion of the behind-the-scenes side of the news organization with which I came into the most frequent contact.

In those days, CBS News provided coverage for the local CBS station, and in fact sent over a news summary every day for me to read on the air. CBS News seemed to acquit itself of its respon- sibility for coverage of New York City with a quick rewrite of the front page of *The New York Times.* Its editor and executives had eyes fixed permanently on the wire machines. Al Morgan once said, "If the Mayor of New York was shot in front of 485 Madison Avenue and a CBS News deskman saw it take place, the first thing he would do would be to rush up to the newsroom on the seventeenth floor and take a look at the AP wire to find out if it had really happened."

As I got to know more and more about CBS News, and my life became more and more closely entwined with it, that original im- pression, going back to the late forties, hung on. Paul White, who had set up the CBS News organization, had been a dynamic, driving newsman, but the best people he hired usually worked their way up to become on-the-air people. What was left to run the place, year after year, stretching right up until the early 1960s, were generally unimaginative ex-newspapermen, hopeless in dealing with news in terms of television.

Part of the problem got right down to dollars, as so many things do. So-called talent—anyone who talked into a microphone (or sang or danced)—was generously rewarded in radio, and, of course, later in TV. A strong union saw to that. Low-level, middle-level, even reasonably high-level managers at CBS were not slaves, in the sense that the pyramids had already been completed, but they were often asked to "manage," to hire and discipline, people making four or five times as much money. Naturally, a news writer with an ounce of ambition fought to get on the air.

This "system"—granted, it was never designed to be a system— had a curious reverse effect on my career. As early as 1952, after the national political conventions in which I had been an active reporter, CBS News showed a firm interest in my becoming a correspondent. I was delighted at the prospect. Successful as my local radio program might be, seven years seemed enough time to have devoted to it. The conventions had shown me that I could compete as a reporter, nose to nose, with the best in the business. I was ready.

The deal never got off the ground. I was offered, as I recall, a base pay of something like $18,000, which was in line with what senior correspondents were getting then. But I was earning about $40,000 a year from WCBS.

I couldn't picture myself going home to the wife and six children and saying, "Honey, I've got good news and bad news. The good news is I'm going to be a CBS News correspondent. The bad news is we're going to starve to death."

Four years later, I took a short leave from *This Is New York* and (by this time) a couple of television programs and covered the 1956 political conventions. Again I was struck with how comfortable I felt as a political reporter on the national scene and how much I wanted to be with CBS News. The script of 1952 was played out again, with the same result. We'd like you, but we can't afford you. By this time I wanted more than ever to move on. But I simply could not afford the salary differential. Once it had seemed that I would never work at CBS at all. But eventually I got there. In 1956 it looked as if I would never be able to join that part of CBS where I truly wanted to be.

The difference between "talent" salaries and management compensation still exists in broadcasting, but pay on the managerial end of the scale has risen enormously, so that top-flight news producers make more than many correspondents. So do some vice presidents. A far cry from the days, twenty-five-odd years ago, when the General Manager of CBS News was paid $25,000 a year.

Somewhere along the march of these years I became interested in politics—as a reporter, not a participant, I hasten to add. As an interviewer I had gotten to know almost all of the important New York political figures, and a few national ones as well. When the timing is right, I soon learned, almost anyone, up to and occasionally including the President of the United States, will appear on a popular program, even a local show. You could drop dead the day after, but when they needed you, they needed you. Of course an interviewer needed important people to talk to every day of the week. Nothing has changed in the guest game in forty years.

As the years went by I became reasonably proficient as an election-night broadcaster, working New York City elections for CBS News. Martin Weldon and Fred Freed became so enamored of politics that they acted as political consultants for a couple of candidates in their spare time, an arrangement that as a CBS News executive in later years I would have forbidden, and properly so.

One beautiful early October day in 1951 Fred Freed and I went to the Polo Grounds and watched Bobby Thomson hit the most famous home run in baseball history, winning the pennant in the last of the ninth for our beloved New York Giants.

When the shouting and the celebrating had quieted down a little, Fred turned to me and said, "I guess these are the good old days."

Years later when, as President of CBS News, I was kept so busy that there almost literally wasn't time to get to the men's room, I asked my old colleague Bud Benjamin why we didn't seem to be having as much fun as we once did. "You're not being paid to have fun," he said. "You're paid to take the heat." True enough.

Perhaps I wasn't being paid to have fun in the old *This Is New York* days, but *fun* is my strongest memory of those years.

4

THE BRAND-NEW DAYS OF TELEVISION

———

In 1984 the Academy of Television Arts and Sciences began putting together a TV Hall of Fame, picking a garland of people each year for sainthood in a medium that hardly existed when World War II ended. Naturally the sidewalks of TV heaven are crowded most heavily with show-business performers (Mary Tyler Moore has won *twenty-nine* Emmys), but three of them are CBS newsmen (Murrow, Cronkite and Sevareid) and two are executives (Stanton and Paley). It was not CBS that got television off the ground; RCA had the most to gain in getting people to watch the new medium: It made television sets.

At the end of the forties, when anyone could see that television would not be a mere novelty any longer, it appeared that RCA–NBC had a very large head start. For some years CBS had kept its foot in the door, operating what was at first an experimental TV station, W2BXA. The station became WCBS-TV, and in early 1947 (by the time I first appeared on television) it was one of four stations programming every day of the week, first only to thousands, eventually to millions in the New York area. Black and white, of course.

A television set then was a very exciting thing to own. One of the best was an RCA console model that projected its image onto a mirror when the lid of the cabinet was elevated 45 degrees. Very fancy indeed.

I was negotiating for a home in the Riverdale section of the Bronx owned by a movie executive who was being transferred to the West Coast. He had one of these up-to-the-minute TV sets, and I had my heart set on it. After the usual haggling, I finally said I would meet his price if he would leave me the TV.

"I couldn't leave that set," he said. "I love it."

"Look," I told him, "for all we know they don't even *have* television on the West Coast yet." (There were eighteen stations in the CBS Television Network up and down the East Coast.)

"You may be right." He laughed, and we shook hands. The house was mine, plus the set, and it wasn't long before I realized how much I hated wrestling.

In the early days of television before time was golden, the problem was this: How does one *fill* time? What does one put before the cameras that will *consume* time? *Lots* of it. All the *good* stuff, almost all the funny men and talented women were over there on radio, where millions could listen and enjoy as they had been doing for generations. Some movies were available, but the TV deals for big movies were years down the road.

There was, of course, no videotape. So live events, *long* live events, were the thing. And, strangely enough, from a technical point of view, television was remarkably sophisticated in what we now think of as its infancy. Cameras were heavy, lights needed patient rigging, cables felt as if you were dragging lead. But everything worked. Television programmers had to get out of studios a good deal of the time because they had so little money with which to do anything *in* studios. As a result, at both networks, a cadre of very able field directors and producers learned the tricks of a trade that had never been a trade before. Their training took place for the first time in coverage of the national political conventions in Philadelphia in 1948. Their handful of viewers saw a preview of what was to come four years later, as television news came of age with gavel-to-gavel coverage of the two great conventions in Chicago in 1952.

But anyone in the news business could understand what Ed Murrow meant when he said he wished television had never been invented. It is difficult enough to be an effective print reporter—to get at the truth, or something like it, and write it all down with clarity. Add one more task for the radio reporter—the extra dimension of voice communications. How to *be* a reporter, stay a reporter and not turn into an announcer. Or, put another way, how to be just enough of a good announcer to communicate your reporting, and not one rounded syllable more. Now try to add the myriad additional complications of television to news reporting and see what it does. The camera, the director, the lights, the film and tape cues, makeup. "Ready to cue Walter." "Cue Walter." It is not for everyone. And it can't *improve* your reporting, can it?

Just as thousands of fine journalists never wished even to add the burden of radio to their professional lives, for fear that it would somehow diminish them, so, particularly in the early days of TV any number of fine newsmen, some at CBS, found television more than they could or cared to handle.

My first time on television I bobbed for apples. One day in 1946 I had a call from Margaret Arlen, hostess of the beautifully titled *Margaret Arlen Show* on WCBS, which followed me on the air every morning. I say beautifully titled because WCBS Radio *owned* not only her show but her *name*. Margaret Arlen was asking me if I would like to be a guest on her television show. I had not known she had a television show, a blissful ignorance I shared with all seven million of my fellow New Yorkers.

"You know where the studios are, don't you, Bill?"

"I'm not exactly sure."

"Grand Central Station. Three o'clock tomorrow. Be there

promptly, because there's makeup, you know, and we go on at three-thirty."

"What will we do?"

"Oh, don't worry about that. The director will think of something. See you tomorrow."

It is not much of a walk from 52nd and Madison to Grand Central Station, but I had left plenty of time. I wondered vaguely whether the studios were next to the famous clock in the middle of the station, off one end of the tracks or somewhere else. *They* turned out to be *one*, a very large soundstage several stories above the station level. I got to know that studio very well indeed over the next couple of decades. From it, with the help of an elevator and a catwalk around the periphery of the great station hall, one could reach the early CBS television newsroom in the Graybar Building.

When I arrived at the studio I was hurried to a corner cubicle where a woman applied heavy makeup, but not as heavy as Miss Arlen's. I barely recognized her under layers of pancake. "Just do what Gil says," she whispered to me, "you'll be fine, we'll have a lot of fun."

"It's sort of dark in here," I observed.

"You just wait."

A canvas pool had been constructed in the center of the studio. A technician was filling it with water from a hose. Low stools were placed around the pool, one for each guest. It looked to me as if the canvas pool would collapse as the water rose higher and higher. The director, a tall, very young man said, "Welcome to television. Now, you are all radio people, and that's fine." I recognized a couple of the other guests. One was Galen Drake, who had another WCBS program. "If this were radio, Miss Arlen could *talk* to you, because I'm sure you're all darn *interesting*. But, you see, this is *television* and it is a *visual*, not an *audible*—I mean it's not primarily an *aural* medium." Gil waited for that to sink in. He was very good at handling children.

"Anyway. What we're going to do is have *fun*." As if on cue, a technician took some rosy red apples out of a bag and threw them into the pool.

"Folks," said Gil, flashing a smile, "the main thing we're going to do on this here TV show is we're going to have a riot *bobbing for apples.*"

We all sat there, too stunned to react.

"That's it. Just like when we were *kids.* Bobbing for apples. On the screen it's going to look *terrific.*"

Gil motioned to another man on the floor.

"May we have lights, please."

The studio instantly went from dusky to ablaze, as if he had turned on a hundred suns. Such light I had never seen or felt. So this was television. In minutes I could feel rivulets of sweat beginning to trickle down my face. One standing light a few yards away seemed to be aimed at my eyes.

A voice shouted, "Thirty seconds to air. Quiet in the studio, please."

We bobbed for apples. Grown men and women, under the baking desert sun of early television lights, chased oversized apples around an artificial pool above Grand Central Station as the early express to Scarsdale got ready to pull out of the bowels of the terminal a hundred feet below.

When it was all over, I went to a bar on Vanderbilt and had a drink. My head was splitting from the effects of the lights. I felt awful. I thought television was a bad joke, if that was any example.

The bartender looked at me with some curiosity. "Excuse me, sir," he said. "Did you just come from the TV?"

"Sure. How did you know?"

"Sir, you have a lot of that makeup all over your face." He handed me a little towel. "That there TV, it sure is something. There's a lot of talk about television these days," he said.

The first television program worthy of the name on which I appeared was a somewhat ambitious and at the same time pathetic attempt to transplant *This Is New York* to the new medium. The station logs bolster my memory and they show that on October 30,

1947, something called *This Is New York* (remote) aired from 6:00 to 7:00 P.M. I remember this was supposed to be the first in a series. It turned out to be the first and last in a series. I recall that we had wanted to show that television could go anywhere and do anything. When we got right down to it, with the limited facilities and money at my disposal, what we could do was bring two or three cameras a few blocks from Grand Central to the New York Telephone Company headquarters and show how the phone system worked. Live. Real nail-biting stuff.

It was not that we did it well, it was that we did it at all. I got the idea that live television was too hot to handle.

At about the time I was making my first fumbling attempts with television, my radio program had become a very solid hit in the New York market. It was for this reason only, I suppose, that I had any opportunities at all to dip a finger into television.

Around WCBS Radio, Arthur Godfrey was the man who had made it big in both media. I could claim early experience, if not success. And experience was at such a premium that on one occasion I was given, along with Douglas Edwards, an entire prime-time evening on television. On very short notice we were told to go to the Grand Central Palace building, where CBS Television's network, stretching at least as far as Philadelphia, would fill the hours with a two-hour prime-time special on the very latest in automobiles.

Doug was stationed on one floor and for fifteen minutes moved along describing cars within range of his cameras and mike. Then he would switch to me, a flight above, and I would go through the same routine with a different set of new models. While I was on the air the cameras and mike cables would be shifted a few hundred feet so that they could take in a whole new part of the floor. When I threw it back to Doug, there he was in a fresh setting. And so it went, up and down, back and forth, car after car, hour after hour. A real draw. *Meanwhile*—in the world of entertainment, over on radio, people were splitting their sides over such nobodies as Jack

Benny, Bing Crosby, Bob Hope, Fred Allen and Edgar Bergen and Charlie McCarthy.

Two hours of prime-time television. Alone, just the two of us, plus an occasional Buick salesman. Enough to turn a fellow's head. Except if you were so silly as to mention that to a neighbor he probably would have said, "We're thinking about getting a television."

In what seemed like one deep breath a television set switched from being a novelty to a necessity. *Douglas Edwards and the News* became a nightly CBS feature, getting under way somewhat later than John Cameron Swayze on NBC. With the help of Fred Freed and others I worked out a reasonably practical way to transform our radio program to television, calling it *Eye on New York*. No money was allotted to it, no decent time period and no sponsors. But it provided a marvelous training ground for me and the others who worked on it. Lewis Freedman, the first director, went on to become a nationally known producer of drama. Lee Hanna rose to be a top-rung television executive. Martin Carr grew into an outstanding documentary film producer whose many credits include the famous documentary *Hunger in America*.

At first *Eye on New York* originated from Liederkranz Hall, a former recital barn on 58th Street between Park and Lexington avenues that CBS had converted for television. Later we moved to the Mansfield Theatre in the Times Square district. In both locations, when we felt too housebound we learned the trick of moving a camera out onto the street and doing a piece there. One I remember was on the subject of dirty streets. The street outside the Mansfield was dirty enough to make the point.

Most of the people on our tiny radio and TV staff were sports fans, and if the occasion came to interview a runner we would move him out onto the street and I would race him on camera for 20 or 30 yards, or try to catch a star pitcher's fastball. You couldn't do that on radio.

We were all sorry that my "fight" with Joe Louis had come before I had a television show to play it on. In the early days of *This Is New*

York, before a Joe Louis fight, someone got the not very bright notion that I should spar with him and report on the air what it felt like to be hit by the greatest fighter of all time.

Joe Louis was well past his prime (it was just before his fight with Ezzard Charles) when I went out to his training camp. Needless to say, I was too. I had not boxed since I was sixteen and had been knocked silly in the second round of an amateur fight in West Hartford, Connecticut. The "bout" was, I suppose, a part of the buildup for the Louis and Charles fight that CBS was scheduled to carry. I guess I had said yes to the ideas as much as anything in the hope that someday down through the years someone would ask me if I had ever done any boxing and I would be able to answer, "Well, a little; I once fought Joe Louis."

As we sat next to each other on the dressing table, anticipation gave way to fright. Stripped to his skivvies, Louis looked absolutely enormous from one end of his body to the other. He caught me with a kind of squinty glance that could have been boredom but that, God forbid, might have been hate. I wondered whether word had reached him that my life was to be spared, that he was to save the real punches for Ezzard Charles.

"Hey, man," he said, not unkindly, "you get in there, don't fcint." Or was it *faint*? I did not dare ask. I said to myself, "Try not to feint or faint." Louis pushed his massive fist into 16-ounce gloves, so big that I could see that if he jabbed me with one of them, which he was certain to do, the glove would cover *all* of my face. I wanted to run and hide. It was too late. It was even too late for men's-room relief, strapped as I was inside an aluminum protector large enough to protect my bottom.

Sugar Ray Robinson and James J. Braddock, great champions, were my "seconds." Robinson said, "Don't hurt him an' he won't hurt you." It didn't seem likely.

Joe Louis and I sparred for two rounds, or rather, he sparred for two rounds. I can remember only that enormous flashing left hand exploding in my face. Between the rounds Braddock said, "You all right?" I nodded, a liar. "Don't you worry none about that left hand, he just keepin' you away from him so you don't get hurt." My head ached for a week from Joe Louis's love taps.

Eye on New York came in many shapes and sizes over the years, and it was a part of the WCBS-TV public-service image long after I had left the station. It won more than its share of awards. But more important, it was a wonderful little experimental laboratory for me, Fred Freed and the others to learn how to handle television.

Interestingly enough, buried as we were in weekend-ghetto time periods and absolutely free of the pressure to produce ratings, the TV broadcast became much more serious than the radio program. I would hardly be stretching a point if I said that we were investigative journalists, although I do not remember that the term was used commonly in those days. We pursued stories, usually New York stories, that we thought were important and tried to translate them into television terms.

One of the things we did with some success on *Eye on New York* was to persuade people to be interviewed on the air against what would seem to be their best interests. It was astonishing how few people would resist the idea of being on television, even if the appearance might make them look foolish or guilty. The correspondents and producers of *60 Minutes*, many years later, count on these same human vanities to get people to appear. Of course we had to do it all live and were desperately constrained by lack of money; the whole program cost only a few hundred dollars a week to produce. But within those constraints we began to learn television journalism in a world where there were no schools, no teachers, indeed no such thing. It was all for the first time.

Early in 1950 I became involved in my first television *news* broadcast. (Let me stop just long enough to note that "broadcast," "program" and "show" are used interchangeably by most people, in and out of the television and radio business. But Frank Stanton felt that "show" and even "program" were words that carried with them strong implications of show business. He felt it was absolutely essential that there be no confusion between news and show business, and therefore he insisted that news product be referred to as "broadcasts." Richard Salant, if not the author of this strict usage, was certainly its vigorous administrator. Personally, I find it a shade unrealistic to confine all news product to the straitjacket of "broadcast." There are religious programs, dramatic programs, documentary programs. So I use "broadcast" and "program" more or less interchangeably in this book and I doubt a soul alive, except Frank or Dick, would argue that there's a difference between the two words. "Show," however, is another matter. The word "show" implies theater and make-believe, the antithesis of what news is or should be all about. I regard it, as Stanton and Salant most certainly would, as improper to use the word "show" in reference to news product, at least news product worthy of the name.)

The agent Jap Gude had at least three clients who needed a little help. One of them was Don Hollenbeck, an enormously talented former foreign correspondent, respected by his colleagues, but suffering under an almost continual barrage of attacks from a New York columnist, Jack O'Brian, for alleged leftist leanings. Another was Tom Meany, a sportswriter of long tooth, sparkling wit and an endless roster of friends. The third was me.

A CBS executive in earlier days, Jap knew everyone in the business and was so generally well regarded that managers sat still and listened when he came up with the idea of a local television news broadcast at six o'clock each night. Strangely enough, in 1950, this was quite a revolutionary idea. How long would it be? No more than fifteen minutes, naturally. People wouldn't sit still for more than fifteen minutes of news, would they? (Today in many cities the evening news locally starts at 4:00 P.M. and goes through till 7:00 P.M. Jap somehow convinced management that he had the three perfect people to do 6 O'Clock Report. Don Hollenbeck with five minutes of hard news, Bill Leonard with an equal amount of feature material and Tom Meany with sports.

The program aired for the first time on Memorial Day 1950. I was the only one of the three men with any television experience and I was an exceedingly busy fellow in those days, with several radio programs in addition to *This Is New York* and *Eye on New York*. So I gave Fred Freed some extra money to help me with the news feature. In his biography, *Special*, Freed gave this account of his first day's work for *6 O'Clock Report*:

A man named Al Gretz and I went out, and since there was no union situation then he carried the camera and I carried the rest of his equipment. The only decision I had made overnight was that our film story would be about the parade. I came up with the idea of telling a story of a little boy watching a parade. I tried to find a little boy with a dog but finally settled on just a little boy, and Al filmed him watching the parade and filmed the parade; and then we rushed the film over to the lab on 11th Avenue and waited until it was processed.

While we waited Al gave me a quick course in shooting and editing film. We then went back to the office and after looking at the film we had shot Al began editing it. I told him the way I thought it ought to look according to the story I had in mind and he made it come out pretty much the way I saw it. Al was a newsreel man and the newsreel style was to cut the film in three-second takes by measuring the amount of film you held between the tip of your nose and the tip of your outstretched hand. As he was cutting and splicing this way I'd sit down at the typewriter and write three seconds of copy. This meant most of our film became a series of nose-to-fingertip, three-second shots, showing the boy's face, the people marching past him, back to the boy, and then another part of the parade.

We rushed the three minutes of virgin film over to the studio and Bill Leonard sat with my script in his hand, looked at the film on a projector and read the copy. We went on the air at six o'clock after only one run-through. Bill had never done anything like that before in his life. None of us had, but it went without a hitch.

Don Hollenbeck's news portion went smoothly, but poor Tom Meany's hand had begun shaking at about four o'clock and hadn't stopped. No wonder. He had never even been on radio before. Meany stumbled through the sports scores in fair style, though, and it looked as if luck was with him until it came time for him to do a live commercial, which local broadcasters were obligated to do. (Hollenbeck, as a CBS correspondent, was excused from this onerous task.) Meany's commercial was for Kool cigarettes. When he came to it, someone on the floor gave him a signal that he did not understand: He thought he was supposed to hurry up with the commercial, so he picked up a package of Kools, tried to shake out a cigarette, had trouble with it, finally shook one free, jammed it in his mouth and lit it. It was a cork-tip Kool, and he lit the wrong end. At the first puff he exploded on camera with a cough heard all the way to Winston-Salem. Through the haze of smoke and the noise of Meany's battle with himself he could be heard to mutter, "Switch from Kools to Hots."

Meany did not last long on the series. He was replaced by a young man with an almost cherubic, open face and a highly professional air style. His name was Jim McKay.

Don Hollenbeck missed—but just barely—being a great CBS newsman, in the Sevareid mold. He wrote with elegance. He cared deeply, perhaps too deeply, about the world and where it might be headed. He was a smooth radio broadcaster, although, like Ed Murrow, Alex Kendrick and a few others, he was suspicious of the network system and where overcommercialization might lead. He was a quiet, lonely, inward man who worried a lot and drank too much—not easy to like. But I came to admire him, first because he showed me what a professional could do to transform ordinary wire-service newscopy into broadcast material that almost seemed to sing. Not by making it more complicated but by somehow making it more simple. He was a *writer*.

Occasionally, Hollenbeck would invite me up to his apartment and we would talk. He had doubts about the new world of television. He had doubts about everything. The continuing red-baiting attacks on him added to his increasing despondency. He began to drink more and more, until his hand would shake holding his script and his good voice would slur. Jack O'Brian's onslaught continued. One day Don missed the broadcast: He had killed himself, a certain victim, in my judgment, of the McCarthy hysteria that swept the country and fouled the nest of radio and television in the early fifties.

This is not the place to recount the Red Channels days, the Army-McCarthy hearings or the famous Murrow broadcast. But no one who worked at CBS in those days could escape the pall of suspicion that was cast, first by Red Channels, then by advertisers, finally by the company itself, on all its talent—writers, producers, broadcasters. We were all asked to sign what amounted to—hell, what *was*—a loyalty oath. CBS was the only network to require such an oath. As far as I can remember, nearly everyone signed, including Murrow and Fred Friendly, who was by this time a very close friend. Like most of my colleagues, I was disgusted with the whole charade, ashamed of CBS for what we all considered to be abject knuckling under . . . but I had nothing to hide. The paper did not say one would be fired for not signing. But . . . I signed.

I drew the line a little later.

There was not only the loyalty oath but a system whereby every guest on my several programs had to be cleared in advance through an appointed CBS executive to make sure he or she was not on a blacklist. One day I invited Oscar Hammerstein up for an interview. He had been a guest several times before, and he and Richard Rodgers had become fairly good friends of mine. To my astonishment, the word came back that Mr. Hammerstein was not cleared. There must be some mistake. No, there was no mistake. Here, Mr. Leonard, is a list of the forbidden organizations that at one time or another Mr. Hammerstein may have contributed to or of which he may even have been a member.

Now I knew I had the sons of bitches.

"Do you know," I said evenly, "that Oscar Hammerstein is the *host* of a great big CBS Network TV special, the whole evening, starring Ethel Merman and Mary Martin? There are ads all over the papers."

"Yes, we know about it."

"Well, you'll have to stop it, won't you?"

"That's a network show, that's none of my business."

"Wait a minute. You mean to say it's all right for Oscar Hammerstein to emcee a tremendous network special in front of the whole country but he can't appear on a crummy local program?"

"I didn't say it was all right. I said the other is none of my business. If you want to know, wise guy, the TV show is an *outside package* and we don't have that much control of talent."

I said, "You're all crazy." If I had been Paddy Chayefsky I would have said, "I'm mad, and I won't take it anymore." I was mad and I wouldn't.

The Rodgers and Hammerstein office was across the street from CBS, at 488 Madison, and I waltzed over and asked for Dick Rodgers. In two minutes I was in his office, telling him the story. If he had shrugged his shoulders, I am sure I would have marched up to see Frank Stanton. But Dick simply said quietly, "What a world. Sit tight. Give me a day or two."

What calls he made I never knew and certainly did not ask. To Paley? Stanton? At any rate, less than forty-eight hours later I was told it would be perfectly okay for me to have Mr. Hammerstein as a guest. It had all been a mistake.

I did not even say thanks. I said I never wanted to be bothered with that guest clearance crap ever again. And I never was.

I was involved with one stimulating radio effort, which I believe later bore fruit in TV. It was called *The New York Story*. It went on the air immediately after a broadcast Ed Murrow and Fred Friendly developed called *Hear It Now*, the direct ancestor of *See It Now*. The two programs, one local and one network, were similar in style—both making full use of crisply edited radio tape. *The New York Story* lacked Murrow and Friendly, but it stood up well, even in their eyes.

By the middle fifties I was literally racing all day, every day, around midtown Manhattan. There were studios everywhere, and a radio or television program to be done in each—at 485 Madison I did two radio broadcasts each week in addition to *This Is New York*; at Grand Central, at West 57th Street and East 58th Street various television activities were the focus of a good deal of my energies. Nothing fails like success, the saying goes, even the kind of small success that I had generated in New York. I was running full out and getting nowhere in particular.

5

CBS REPORTS – WITH MURROW AND FRIENDLY

Fred Friendly is a serious journalist with a Hollywood personality, and that confuses friends and enemies alike. He is a dragon-slayer who outroars the dragons.

With Fred every moment is a great discovery he cannot wait to share. He bursts upon each fact, each idea as if it were his own and often gives it new bounce because of the sheer energy and passion he pours into it. In recent years he has discovered the Constitution of the United States, a large enough hunk of material for him to sink his teeth into, and, by God, he has shaken it up and made it more alive to thousands of students and viewers. He is some piece of work.

I fell under his spell in the late 1950s, and my life has not been the same since. Indeed, without him I might never have departed New York radio and television for the wilder network shores, and my home phone might never have rung in the middle of one night in 1960.

"Hello, Bill, it's Fred."

"I know who it is, Fred. No one else calls at four in the morning. What's going on?"

"Bill. Listen to me. Are you awake?" Not waiting for an answer: "Water! Say 'water' to me when you get in in the morning."

"'Water'?"

"That's right. 'Water.'"

"Fred, for God's sake."

"I didn't mean to disturb you."

Stunned silence.

"I'll just leave you with this thought. There isn't enough water. The world is running out. It's going dry. I've been reading all night. Think about it."

Fred Friendly had discovered water, as he had discovered, or would discover, the perils of smoking, the evils of bookmaking, the plight of migrant workers, the rights of blacks, the mind of Walter Lippmann, the dangers of bad driving and the glory of the Supreme Court. In his insatiable drive to translate into television what he thought important and controversial, Fred plunged headlong into just about everything except the Holy Roman Church, and I have a hunch if he had lasted long enough at CBS he might have gotten around to that.

When Fred Friendly discovered something it generally stayed discovered, usually with the not inconsiderable help of Edward R. Murrow, although the worldwide water shortage defied even his efforts to bring it to its knees. The late David Lowe, one of the original *CBS Reports* producers, once said to me, only half in jest, "I'm afraid the son of a bitch has got 'legend' written all over him." That was in 1960. It is more than two decades since Friendly left CBS News but the corridors and the columns still bubble with Friendly quotes. He remains vivid and controversial years after he tilted at his last windmill.

Fred and I originally met and had been drawn together because Jap Gude, the agent we shared, liked both of us. Over lunch at Louis and Armand's, Jap would tell me about this remarkable fellow named Friendly who was probably going to go with NBC. Fred and I were interested in the same kind of documentary radio and television, we happened to live only a few blocks apart in Riverdale and we were both Murrow men, Fred professionally, beginning with a record album they put together, and I at least in spirit and admiration.

At a particularly difficult time in my life Fred went far out of his way to be helpful. In October 1956, at the age of forty, I had a fairly severe heart attack. I was in the hospital for nearly six weeks, unable to continue my radio or television programs, certainly for months, and, for all I knew at the time, perhaps forever. By this time my first wife and I had separated and I was living in Manhattan, my income as well as my health somewhat less than blossoming.

It was just about this time that Murrow and Friendly began their historic *See It Now* series. Alcoa was the sole sponsor of the series, and somehow Fred controlled the tone, if not the precise copy, of the commercials, which were voice-over-film footage. Fred felt that it did not befit the dignity of his broadcasts for a commercial announcer to be "selling" on them, no matter how subdued the copy, but staff news correspondents were not then, and, properly, are not now, permitted to do commercials. I provided a convenient solution. A newsman—well, yes. But commercials were, as they still are, a part of a local broadcaster's life. Fred suggested that I do the commercials. The problem was that I was too ill to leave my apartment. I imagine that someone at the agency said at that point, "Well, the hell with that, let's get somebody who can at least get to the studio." But if so they reckoned without Friendly. He let it be known that Leonard was the man he wanted, and that was that. One morning a CBS engineer and a dolly loaded with audio gear arrived at my door. I did the commercials. I don't know whether it was good for Alcoa but it was good for my bank account and my morale, in no particular order.

Coronaries were taken even more seriously thirty years ago than they are today, perhaps because doctors knew so much less about what to do to prevent the next one. I must have indicated to my doctor at one point in the recuperation period that I assumed my life was pretty much over. Dr. Mason Hicks laughed and said, "Nonsense, I've known people who've had heart attacks and lived up to twenty years."

I asked him for his advice. "Just one thing," he said. "Never smoke another cigarette as long as you live." Pretty good advice in 1956. I took it. By then the link between cigarettes and lung cancer had been reasonably well established, but Dr. Hicks's certainty that tobacco was bad for the heart was somewhat ahead of his time.

I survived, but my strength was not back to full throttle for the better part of a year. Although it was a time that might have appeared even to friends to have been a low point of my life ("Poor Bill, not hardly forty, is he?") it was actually the very springtime of a new life personally and, as it turned out, professionally.

Early in 1957 I agreed to the divorce my first wife had sought, and in May that year Kappy Wallace and I were married. I was no great prospect. Not only was I in questionable health, but also I brought with me the part-year responsibility for six young boys, five sons and a stepson, ranging in age from four to sixteen—as my mother once said, "the triumph of carelessness over common sense."

After our wedding we set out upon our honeymoon to a lakeside cottage near Goshen, New York, lent by a friend. Some honeymoon: Kappy and I and *eight* boys—for with us also were her two sons, Peter and Chris, who soon became as close to me as any of my own. Peter Wallace, her eldest, died in Greece in a mountain-climbing accident in 1962. Chris Wallace has grown up to be a successful television journalist. My youngest son, Oliver, is also in television, as an editor at CBS News. But I am more relieved than disappointed that the other boys have branched out into other forms of enterprise. Will Leonard, my eldest, is an accountant in Florida, Andrew and Nicolas both live in California and work in computers and communications, respectively. James is an environmentalist who lives in Hawaii. So we have the U.S.A. fairly well blanketed.

The last time Kappy and I counted up our grandchildren we got a grand total of fifteen. A grand total indeed.

During the previous winter, trying to find my lost health under a warm sun, I had taken a leisurely trip to the Caribbean, an excursion that had a curious bearing on the rest of my career. In the course of my convalescence I received a get-well call from Red Smith, a fine sportswriter and a good friend. He mentioned that he would soon be in the Dominican Republic, where four terrific ball players, all named Alou, came from, and anyway he liked it there. I changed my plans a bit and agreed to meet up with him.

Red Smith and I both stayed where almost everyone else stayed, at the El Embajador Hotel just outside the capital city, which was then called Ciudad Trujillo. It was a pretty fair hotel, by the standards of those days, with a golf course, swimming pool and a nice crooked casino run by a little man from Memphis with the perfect name for a casino manager, Jack Slot. Red and I went around to a fourth-rate little ballpark to watch two of the Alou brothers play and to the cockfights to watch a few chickens destroy each other. Everywhere we went the conversation got around to Trujillo, and how he ran the country with an iron fist, how he was worse than Hitler and had certainly lasted a lot longer. Red Smith said he guessed if there were trains in the Dominican Republic he would have them running on time, except during siesta.

We had not been in Ciudad Trujillo very long before we were given a demonstration of the dictator's delicate touch that convinced us both that he really ran the place. The country's so-called Director of Sports had been personally assigned to Smith, who was recognized as a man who could do things for the DR. Red and I both loved the horses, and he asked the Director if the racetrack was open and if so could we arrange a visit? The answer came back, no, the track wasn't open, but wait, if El Benefactor ordered a special one-day meeting then it *would* be open, *comprende?* The Director asked to be excused. Red Smith offered me one-to-five on a special one-day meeting. I told him no takers, and sure enough the next day the man came back, all smiles, with the word that El Benefactor himself would be at the track for the special one-day meeting day after tomorrow honoring the distinguished Rojo Smith.

When we got to the track Red said, "I wonder if he can make the horses run on time?"

They had put together four races on short notice, and before the first race we were led into a box and introduced to Trujillo, who gave us a hard handshake and left almost immediately, not waiting even for the ratty-looking horses to parade onto the track. When they did, a man who was part of our escort party came up and pressed a slip of paper into our hands. On it were written four numbers. Red and I compared notes. The first was number 5, and sure as sunrise number 5 won the first. So it went. The right number for the second and the third. We had bet very little. Our host was annoyed. "Why you no bet more?" Red Smith said, "It's against my religion." After the fourth race we thanked our host and told him to please thank El Benefactor for staging the races. I said to Red, "You realize, this whole country is on the fix."

The racetrack scene was preposterous, and in its way hilarious, but it provided me with the germ of an idea. Here, in our own backyard, was absolute dictatorship personified—the same power that could fix a race could snuff out thousands of human lives—and had done so. I thought about it, and never quite forgot it. It was Trujillo and the Dominican Republic that led me to *CBS Reports*.

In 1959 *CBS Reports* was salvaged from the wreckage of the Murrow-Friendly *See It Now* series, which had broken new ground in documentary television journalism over the previous two years. It began, of course, with the famous pair of shots with which Ed Murrow asked director Don Hewitt to punch up pictures, simultaneously, of the Atlantic and then the Pacific Ocean, as if to say, we can and will go anywhere, in a hurry, and do anything. Not by any means was every *See It Now* broadcast controversial—a few of them, in fact, were remarkably soft—but when *See It Now* got down to cases it was tough and uncompromising.

Remember, this was a medium still feeling its way, learning what it could do, what it could be. What Murrow and Friendly did with *See It Now* was to make people uncomfortable every once in a while. To make it impossible just to sit back, relax and enjoy it, to be shaken to the point of sitting up and taking notice. Uncomfortable. Uncomfortable for sponsors. For affiliates. For CBS. *See It Now's* most uncomfortable broadcast was its greatest, and perhaps the single most influential program of television history. In it Ed Murrow did what President Eisenhower failed to do—he personally challenged and, with all the power of television at his back, helped destroy Senator Joseph McCarthy.

His unwitting collaborators were the stations of the CBS Television Network, some of whom were uneasy or downright unhappy after the fact. Paley and Stanton knew something about the broadcast in advance, and gave at least lip-service support to Murrow after it. But in spite of generally favorable public reaction, "uncomfortable" would be too mild a word to describe their relationship with Ed Murrow at about that time. And if *See It Now* was a succès d'estime, it was a failure by the standards of men who run networks. Its ratings were weak. Its only sponsor, Alcoa, decided not to renew and there was no other in the wings. The final break between Ed and CBS was still a couple of years down the road, but *See It Now*, representing the very best of which CBS News was capable, was finished.

I knew next to nothing about the struggle to try to save something from the wreckage of *See It Now*. I say "next to nothing" because as my health returned and I moved back into the swim of local radio and television work, I found myself informally drawing closer to Friendly, and I remember a lunch in which Fred, with his flair for understatement, almost sobbed, "It may get to the point where I'll be coming to you for a job."

In the aftermath of the quiz scandals of 1958, Stanton was committed to some prime-time documentaries, regardless of the fate of *See It Now*. Although Ed Murrow's role was sharply curtailed, a unit called *CBS Reports* was created, with Friendly as executive producer. It would turn out six prime-time documentaries the first year (1959–1960), more in subsequent years. Murrow would narrate some but not all of them.

No one said it, but the Murrow years at CBS News were to all intents over, and the Friendly years—few as they would be—had begun.

Where *See It Now* had been primarily a Murrow broadcast, with Ed front and center, *CBS Reports* would be much more a producer's program, serious documentaries all, with narrator less important than subject matter. *CBS Reports* would have to give way to soft cultural documentaries in almost half the prime-time periods allocated to CBS News. It was in this somewhat us-against-the-world atmosphere that Friendly gathered most of the troops who had fashioned *See It Now* and prepared to turn out documentaries that did not necessarily depend on Edward R. Murrow.

Fred was an extraordinary producer and editor who put his broadcasts together in a fashion that might charitably be described as haphazard. He seldom went into the field to investigate a story or work with a film crew, preferring to dispatch men who were referred to as producers, although, in fact, Friendly was the producer for all his own broadcasts. He went about it all at an undisciplined, explosive pace, driving his troops beyond all that was reasonable, as so many good generals do.

Though he had never shot a foot of film, he seemed to have been born in the editing room. He had a superb gift for taking one of his producer's efforts, immediately spotting what was wrong, quickly rearranging, rewriting or dispatching him for reshooting, and somehow coming up with what both of them really had in mind all along. He was alternately illogical and perceptive, shrewd and naive. He had, and still has, a remarkably keen "feel" for what's going on in the world, of where attention should be paid. The day after I went to work for *CBS Reports* in 1959, I asked Gene DePoris, one of his producers, what it was like working for Friendly. "Usually I want to kill him," he said. "But, you know, that's Fred."

Friendly was scrounging around for good ideas for the new *CBS Reports* when I began to talk about Trujillo and what a documentary

he and his comic-opera country might make. Fred asked me if I
thought I had any chance of getting an interview with the old man,
and I said I thought the only way would be to make a major invest-
ment in time and effort—that is, show the Dominicans that we
were really serious about documenting their country, and then
when they were used to seeing us around perhaps we could get to
Trujillo, although, admittedly, no American television journalist
ever had. Fred asked me if I wanted to try to implement this,
provided we could work out a deal whereby I became a CBS News
correspondent and producer whose main assignment was *CBS Reports*. I said I would jump at the chance.

The time and the circumstances were just right. The move from
WCBS to CBS News that had almost happened on two other occasions over nearly seven years finally took place, thanks in large
measure to Fred.

What I knew about making 35mm film documentaries at the
time I set out for the Dominican Republic could fit on the head of a
pin and still leave room for the Lord's Prayer. Fred Freed and I had
shot a good many short pieces on 16mm film for *Eye on New York*
and *6 O'Clock Report*; the transition from editing radio tape to
editing film seemed to have come naturally to me. I felt I was pretty
good at it, at least in dealing with brief pieces, and somehow I just
assumed that I could make the transition into longer form. The bliss
of the ignorant. And I do not recall any apprehension at the thought
of what might happen to my career if I spent months in the Dominican Republic and failed to deliver.

To this day, in fact, I remember my sense of confidence that I was
a good enough reporter to find the Trujillo story and cover it—why
be concerned about a little obstacle like not knowing the language? I
simply recognized that here was an opportunity that might make my
professional life blossom, just as marriage to Kappy had done for my
personal life.

I had extensive preparation for the first of my *CBS Reports* programs. It began with a meeting with Palmer Williams, Friendly's

deputy, an island of sanity in a sea of madness, to whom I complained that I had not been able to corner Fred for detailed instructions since we had decided to go ahead with the Trujillo project.

"That figures," said Palmer. "Why don't you just go? After you have a chance to look around and figure out what you want to shoot, just let me know and I'll send you Marty Barnett and his assistant, plus Larry Gianneschi for sound. That'll be your crew. They're a good bunch." The phone rang on his desk, and he was shortly deep in another conversation. Finally I waved at him. He put his hand over the phone. "Good luck. Keep in touch."

Before leaving for the Dominican Republic, I did manage to corner Fred. He looked at me earnestly, as if I were the only person in the world who meant anything to him; for a moment perhaps I was. "Good luck," he whispered. "We're counting on you. Ed and I."

The men who filmed documentaries from the 1950s to the early 1960s came almost without exception from the ranks of the old newsreel cameramen, and a number of them—Leo Rossi, Charley Mack, Marty Barnett among them—formed the core of professionals who brought the television documentary to its first flowering. The 35mm camera they used was heavy and hard to handle. It needed to be fed with an inordinate amount of light, and the lights themselves were bulky and hot. In comparing the mobility of a print journalist with the immobility of his television counterpart, Friendly would sometimes say to television columnists that we "carried a thousand-pound pencil." This was an exaggeration, but not a wild one.

Black box after black box full of lights, shades, lenses, batteries, amplifiers, cables, tripods, handhelds and assorted spares filled a couple of station wagons and/or a small plane. The 12-volt storage battery that drove the camera motor was usually hand-carried onto a plane and occupied its own first-class seat (this was to make sure the battery acid did not spill all over our luggage). By union contract, camera crews flew first class at all times; correspondents were not always that lucky. I remember flying once from Cairo to Kenya in the back of a plane while a camera crew and a 12-volt battery flew up front. I didn't like it then and, thinking it over a quarter of a century later, I don't like it now.

By today's standards, the old 35mm equipment was clumsy and comparatively immobile. But the quality of the pictures turned out by those 35mm cameramen was very fine indeed. The film, of course, was black-and-white.

True to his word, Palmer Williams sent cameraman Marty Barnett, his assistant Harry Elatkin and soundman Larry Gianneschi down to the Dominican Republic. I had prepared a long list of innocuous scenes and events to film that would show the palace spies who kept me under observation that CBS really wanted to film what a lovely, happy place old Trujillo had down there.

In the meantime, I'd begun to learn a little about shooting 35mm film in the field. I also kept requesting an interview with Trujillo, but the closest I got was the chance to film his Secretary of State, Manuel De Moya.

We set up our equipment in De Moya's home, a place that would put the ordinary Beverly Hills mansion to shame. De Moya was a handsome, smooth and quite charming fellow in his mid-fifties who spoke an excellent brand of English, and it wasn't easy to believe the stories that he was high in the chain of minions who saw to it that Trujillo took 20 percent off the top of everything.

While De Moya was explaining how the countless stories about Trujillo had all been planted by Fidel Castro and were really directed against the United States, we came to the end of a reel. Marty Barnett stopped everything while he changed film, and Larry Gianneschi asked De Moya if it was possible for him to use the facilities. De Moya waved a gracious, aristocratic hand indicating they were down the hall and on the left. When Larry came back, his face was pale. He bent over and whispered to me, "Jesus Christ, there's a fucking submachine gun hanging behind the door in there." I excused myself a few minutes later to take a look, and sure enough, there it was—an Israeli machine pistol. The fact was, as I learned quickly, that carrying arms, concealed or otherwise, was a way of life among the tiny clique ruling the Dominican Republic. These men were painfully aware of the thousands who had suffered under El Benefactor and were waiting for a chance to get even.

During our stay, the tension was palpable, although the closest thing I saw to an assassination attempt was nothing more than a blob of red paint splashed on one of the hundreds of huge poster portraits of the dictator that constituted most of the public art in and around the capital. Less than three years later, however, the inevitable happened: Trujillo was gunned down.

All dictatorships are fundamentally alike, so much so that it is fruitless to spend much time comparing them. But for sheer rigidity of one-man rule, for sheer cruelty, for nepotism on a grand scale, it would be hard to beat the example of Rafael Trujillo, who ran his country for thirty-one years, amassing a fortune in the hundreds of millions, and left in his wake a grisly trail of torture and murder. Trujillo's Dominican Republic was particularly fascinating because it was so close to our shores, its people so attractive, its scenery so engaging, and because it was small enough for a reporter to observe, almost at a glance, precisely how a dictatorship works—and does not work.

When we went down to film the Trujillo documentary the American newspapers were full of stories about the murder of a man named Galindez, supposedly at the hands of Trujillo's people. All the old Trujillo horror tales were trotted out again. Ciudad Trujillo was a dicey place to visit, especially for an American reporter, and indeed Trujillo was having a difficult time attracting visitors of any sort. He had hired a succession of American public relations firms to improve his image and sell tourism, and his influence peddling even extended into the ranks of the U.S. Congress, where it included a friendly relationship with then Senator George Smathers of Florida. But none of his efforts succeeded in drawing folks to a place that they kept reading abounded in missing persons, torture and good stuff like that.

Consequently, the El Embajador Hotel and the nearby multimillion-dollar exhibition area just being completed were sadly lacking in that essential ingredient for a prosperous tourist economy: tourists. Which was a shame, because it was a lovely place to visit. I had a splendid sunny room on a high floor. In one direction I could see a bit of the Caribbean. In the other I looked across a polo field, where one of Trujillo's sons romped with his hard-riding playmates once or twice a week, and beyond it to a golf course. (A few years later it became the bivouac area for the Marines when the U.S. went in to keep the place safe for democracy.)

Before leaving the U.S. I had asked for permission to operate a ham radio station during my stay in the Dominican Republic, and to my surprise I was granted a license. I took along a small but quite powerful transceiver, which I set up in my room. Naturally, I was concerned that the authorities would think I was using the radio for spying or sending secret messages, so I decided to go right to the lion in his den and ask for help in fastening the end of an antenna wire to a light stanchion. A heavyset goon from Trujillo's secret police, José Carbonel, had been assigned to "look after me," and I made a point of showing him the radio gear, explaining that I had a proper license and asking for his help in getting a boy to scramble up the stanchion.

"By the way, Joe," I laughed, "let me know if this interferes with any of the bugging equipment your people have put in the room."

"They are not my people," replied Carbonel solemnly. "Not to worry."

In the course of several months we filmed just about everything in the Dominican Republic—except the booming economy El Benefactor's press agent kept talking about, for indeed there wasn't any. By engaging a separate room and somehow dodging José Carbonel, I even managed to film several interviews with underground activists right in the hotel. But I didn't seem to be getting any closer to that Trujillo interview I craved.

I had just about given up when word came that we were to go to a certain ranch outside of town, set up our equipment in the stable area and *perhaps* be able to film Trujillo there. Sure enough, after a short wait, the great dictator, in a cowboy outfit, rode into range on a white horse. He dismounted. Manuel De Moya hove into sight to act as interpreter, and I launched into the first and last interview Trujillo gave to U.S. television.

It was not so much what he said but that he said it at all. Predictably, he placed the blame for most of the troubles in the Caribbean right at the doorstep of Fidel Castro. His interview turned out to have been peppered with swear words that shocked a lot of people who understood Spanish, but they sailed over my head at the time.

I realized that my gamble and Fred Friendly's had paid off. We had Trujillo. Probably the rest of the documentary would pale compared to the dazzling sight of El Benefactor, dressed in a white riding outfit, as if he were ready to star in a Hollywood western, riding forth on his white stallion. And it did turn out that way.

Of course, in addition to the interview with El Benefactor, I wanted to find, report on and film some of the underground opposition to Trujillo. Thanks to ham radio, that turned out to be easy. I soon met an American named John Delles, a local businessman who shared my interest in ham radio and golf. One day on the golf course, I found out from John that one of his wife's relatives was active in the anti-Trujillo movement. From then on, one contact led to another.

It was on that same golf course that I met a young man who was to become one of my closest friends, Claus von Amsberg, who was then second, perhaps third, secretary in the West German embassy. Claus was very anti-Trujillo and well-tuned to what was going on at the palace, at the embassies, in the underground movement. On the last day of my stay, when I was sailing very close to the wind, with the authorities finally aware that I had been talking to and filming the opposition, Claus called me to say that I was about to be arrested, that I had better hurry and get out of the country. An hour or so later, with the personal escort of our ambassador, Joseph Farland, the film crew and I got to the airport, one step ahead of Trujillo's henchmen.

I did not see Claus again until several years later, when Kappy and I ran into him while we were waiting for a table at a Chinese restaurant on upper Broadway. He was with his bride, Princess (now Queen) Beatrix of the Netherlands. Almost every year since that meeting we have exchanged visits, most often in Italy, and we have watched their three boys grow from cradle to manhood. I suppose I have Trujillo—or should it be Fred Friendly?—to thank for a fine, enduring friendship.

Friendly had that instinct to go to the dramatic heart of any subject matter. Whenever a producer would come back from shooting a documentary, he'd say, "Show me a scene." By this he would mean something memorable, memorable to us and maybe to the people who watched television. Ed Murrow standing by the yawning hatch covers of the Polaris missile submarines in "Biography of a Missile" was one such scene. Trujillo on his horse was another.

Nailing down Trujillo nailed down my job at *CBS Reports*. In March 1960 "Trujillo: Portrait of a Dictator" went on the air. I had finally narrated, written and produced a *CBS Reports* prime-time documentary.

"Trujillo" was by no stretch of the imagination the best of the many excellent documentaries turned out by Friendly and his people in the first year of *CBS Reports*, but it did win the Ed Stout Award for Outstanding Foreign Reporting, and it made me feel I had finally broken out of the *This Is New York* mold. I was quickly off on a succession of other documentary projects, some of which I anchored and produced alone. But in 1961, when Fred and I decided to tackle the subject of the inequities of the American ballot box, Fred felt the subject was so difficult to bring to life that he needed to use the stirring voice and presence of Ed Murrow to keep people from dropping off to sleep early. I was hurt at being shunted aside by a relief pitcher, even if he was the greatest of all time, when I'd just gotten used to going all nine innings alone, but Fred did the right thing.

Years later, on more than one occasion, I made the same kind of decision, cutting into the ego of a totally involved producer who simply could not understand why I insisted on a star correspondent to provide the narration when the producer had done 99 percent of the work. The reason, in both cases, was that viewers tend to believe material from someone they recognize, trust and respect. If the material is so extraordinary it sells itself, it doesn't much matter who the narrator is or how professional, or even, in rare cases, whether there *is* a narrator. But when in doubt, my instant thought was: Let's use Cronkite if he's available.

There were some very fine field producers on the old *CBS Reports* staff, among them Joe Wershba, David Lowe, Gene DePoris and Arthur Morse. They were considerably better than I. I was— and still am—far more comfortable, and make a larger contribution, in the editing room and at a typewriter. In the field I think too much as a reporter and not enough as a filmmaker. The best producers get out there and somehow manage to do both.

David Lowe's classic "Harvest of Shame" and perhaps too "Biography of a Missile" seem to be the only early *CBS Reports* documentaries that have a life of a quarter century or more. But most, if not all, of the documentaries produced by Friendly and his group in the early sixties stand the test of time well, reflecting subject matter of importance and reporting of substance.

The *CBS Reports* team operated in a world different from that inhabited by the rest of CBS News, just as the *60 Minutes* group does today. Many of the producers, cameramen and film editors were not even known by name to the rest of the organization. The CBS Television News people worked out of the Grand Central area for years, and never met the *CBS Reports* team, whose mission was far different. Ed Murrow, of course, had access everywhere, but he was an increasingly distant figure in all parts of CBS News by the late 1950s. Curiously, except for Friendly himself, I was the only *CBS Reports* staff member who was generally known throughout CBS News. I had done a great many news broadcasts of one sort or another; I had worked the political conventions and elections; I knew virtually all the managers and correspondents. In fact, I knew much more about CBS and CBS News at the working level than Fred did.

Perhaps for that reason, and perhaps too because he respected my judgment, I became a kind of unofficial consultant to him on a variety of matters. In an odd way, I had been "out in the world" considerably more than he. He would question me closely about things and people, and try out his ideas on me. I was always frank with him. He didn't seem to mind when I'd say, "Fred, that's bullshit." Not everyone had that kind of relationship with Fred Friendly.

6

THE
GREAT
ELECTION GAME

Most turns in most careers are accidental, at least in part, and this was true of my deep involvement in CBS News coverage of politics, particularly coverage of the political conventions and elections.

In recent years, CBS News has been generally so preeminent among the network organizations that not everyone recalls the considerable period of time when it ran second to NBC News. This was in the days, beginning in 1957, when Chet Huntley and David Brinkley were dominant in the early evening television news ratings. The NBC team outdrew Walter Cronkite for a number of years after he took over from Douglas Edwards.

The Huntley-Brinkley magic worked for NBC News in its coverage of the 1960 political conventions, swamping CBS News in the ratings on election night. In those days, convention and election coverage seemed to set the tone for audience preference in news for months, even years afterward. In spite of great faith in Cronkite, who was gaining in stature and performance with each passing year, CBS News was lagging uncomfortably behind in television, and television was now the name of the game.

Top management at CBS News was, to say the least, in transition at about this time, Dick Salant having replaced Sig Mickelson as President. General Manager was Blair Clark, a thoughtful, considerate man who had been a radio correspondent in Paris but who was not precisely suited to his management role. The man really in charge was the blunt, uncompromising Ernest Leiser. He too had been a radio correspondent, but he was cut from a different cloth. He was not loath to manage.

After our coverage of the New York City election in 1961, in which we lagged far behind NBC, Leiser decided that elections and conventions needed full-time attention. He approached Salant with the idea of starting an election and convention unit, with a single executive producer in full charge of coverage of all political special events and broadcasts. Leiser got an immediate go-ahead. My name came up for the top job.

Obviously, the job had its dangers. There had never been anything like a semiautonomous political coverage group at any news division before. It was anyone's guess whether or not it would help our performance in this area. Would a specially created authority be given the muscle not only to plan but to execute coverage of conventions and elections? If so, would correspondents and producers, to say nothing of the management that had created it, follow willingly whatever new paths might be carved out? I talked to Blair Clark and Ernie Leiser. They both said they hoped I would take the job. I said I would let them know. One or two close friends warned me against it. They said I already had a perfect job as a working producer and correspondent, for which I had worked so hard, that I would be giving it up to take potluck as some "executive" in an area where CBS News was up against an unbeatable team. It didn't make any sense, they said.

In spite of all that good advice, I didn't hesitate for long. Friendly advised that I insist on reporting directly to Blair Clark, and I was determined to do some air work occasionally and keep my status as a CBS correspondent. I made both of these conditional to my acceptance, and Clark agreed.

Far from being apprehensive about the challenge, I was innocent enough to look forward to it.

Of all the CBS correspondents, Walter Cronkite was perhaps closest to me. We had hit it off well personally as far back as 1952, when he first anchored a convention and I was a floor reporter. Whether Walter had had anything to do with the job offer I did not know, but I was sure he would approve of it. In fact, as soon as my appointment was announced, he called to tell me so. "I hear you're going to be my boss," he said cheerily. "That's great!"

"I should live so long, Walter," I said. "But many thanks." Neither of us, of course, could foresee that two and a half years later we would be involved in a major eruption, stemming from the fact that I actually tried to *be* his boss, neither wisely nor too well.

Ernie Leiser had a large stake in the success of the election unit, which was formed in the waning days of 1961. "I'm going to give you," he said a little sourly, as if they were being torn from his ribs, "two of the best men in the whole damn news division. You're going to need all the help you can get." He was right on both counts.

The men were William Eames and Robert Wussler. Eames, the older of the two, was a pleasant round-faced man who had a level head, one arm, and who always seemed to be about to burst out laughing. He made an immediate excellent impression on just about everyone and as a result was constantly being offered jobs both inside and outside the company. Eventually, one of these offers took him to Los Angeles, where he spent many years as a news director and broadcaster. From there he went to Washington for the CBS-owned television stations. But before all that, Bill Eames was a key member of our election unit.

Bobby Wussler, then only twenty-five, was already a television news production veteran, having caught on at CBS while still in his teens. He had a driving energy, a high competitive spirit, a flair for organization and affection for and understanding of all the paraphernalia of television. The young Bobby Wussler had some rough edges that went with his obvious abilities, and there were some at CBS who felt he pushed too hard, too fast, but I liked him and did my best to contain his energies and keep them sensible.

Bobby was a tireless worker, fun to work with and fun to play with, and whatever success the election unit enjoyed was in great measure thanks to him. Eventually, he became head of the election unit himself, and in 1972, he took off on a roller-coaster career that in a few short years saw him become General Manager of WBBM-TV in Chicago, Vice President of CBS Sports and then for a short time President of the CBS Television Network. In recent years he has been Executive Vice President of Turner Broadcasting.

We were joined by a genial top sergeant, Al Thaler, the kind of fellow who could find cold beer in the Sahara. I thought we ought to have a researcher; as far as I knew there was only one at CBS News, a curious little man named Stan Merkin. I managed to corral him. Merkin said he would work for us if he could keep the hours he was used to—that is, coming in *very* early in the morning ("When everything is quiet and I can get my work done") and leaving early in the afternoon. I don't know why I said yes to this nonsensical arrangement. Actually, instead of leaving in midafternoon, Merkin would beat it when everyone else was at lunch.

Eventually I learned that he was running an antique store in upper Westchester County. By the time he quit a few years later to devote full time to his customers, Research had become a major department of CBS News, embracing scores of young men and women and providing one of the major stepping-stones into the ranks of producers. But a cadre of researchers—to say nothing of a film archive worthy of the name—simply did not exist at the time the election unit began.

In 1961 the offices of CBS News were still scattered over most of Manhattan, or so it seemed. Most of the management team and all of the radio division operated out of 485 Madison Avenue, television news from the Graybar Building, Fred Friendly's group from a building on the corner of Ninth Avenue and 47th, Bud Benjamin's *20th Century* program from the cutting rooms on West 45th Street and a team that turned out cultural documentaries from offices in the old Sheffield milk plant on West 57th Street. In 1963 everyone moved into the West 57th Street location, which brought the divisions together overnight. Many CBS News people who had never met each other before were now introduced. I cannot overemphasize the importance of the move that finally brought the various elements of CBS News together under one roof. But that was still in the future.

Space was tight and I was lucky: My group wasn't assigned quarters somewhere in Queens. Instead, we were told to make ourselves as comfortable as possible in Studio 2, on the 21st floor of 485 Madison, a large high-ceiling soundproof radio studio where I had worked many hundreds of times. Once I'd had a modest celebrity interview show on the CBS Radio Network, *In Town Today*, no smash hit, I'm afraid, and there I'd been one day in Studio 2 interviewing Danny Kaye. For some reason we were not sitting down at a table but standing on opposite sides of a mike. As we began to talk, Danny began to tilt the mike and to tilt along with it. I followed suit. In a few seconds I found myself asking questions from the uncomfortable angle of 45 degrees. Danny was smiling, winking, making faces. In answer to a question he said, "My dear Bill, would you be more comfortable if we were both lying flat on the floor?" Gently he lowered the mike stand all the way down, and we continued the interview from there. Danny was so pleased with himself and the problems he was causing me and our audio engineer that he began playing a kind of hide-and-seek with the mike stand. It was all I could do to stay within range. When it was finally over he said, "I haven't had so much fun with an interview in years." I always thought of it later as my Danny Kaye studio.

I made my office in what had been the old control room. A large window of soundproof glass looked out over the big studio, where once the CBS orchestra had played in the glamour days of radio. Now that kind of radio was finished forever.

The very first decision I made on my new job was one of the most important in my career—and quite a significant one for CBS News, although it was taken rather casually at the time, with no real sense of what its impact would be. It was to make the computers we used real tools instead of toys.

Since the beginning days of radio in the early 1920s and on into the era of television, the networks performed what was considered to be a useful and complete service on election night. Basically, it amounted to reporting wire-service and newspaper coverage of the election. The speed of our returns was limited to the speed with which the two wire services added up the votes released by various counties, cities or parts of cities throughout the nation. The commentary of shrewd political reporters and politicians, their eye on favorite key precincts, supplemented the raw voting information we offered our audience.

As early as 1956, computers had been used on election-night broadcasts. "Displayed" might be the better word. They constituted a kind of electronic freak show, spitting out odds and predictions that no one took very seriously. The impression on the person watching at home was that the computer was part of a guessing game, but somehow it wasn't amusing; it was damned confusing. Was IBM's computer right when it predicted so early in the evening that John F. Kennedy was favored 100 to 1 to be the next President? Maybe not. At the very least, the computers and their funny predictions gave reporters something to chuckle about early in the evening before the votes had begun crashing in and things got serious. We all assumed the people watching election returns found it equally amusing. Besides, the computer companies had given the networks all those hundreds of thousands of dollars' worth of machines (and the people to run them) for nothing, and they livened up the set.

The first target of the new election unit was the off-year national elections of 1962, in which a whole new House and a third of the Senate were at stake. My mission seemed reasonably simple: to tell viewers who had won and to inform them sooner than any other network. One could count on the CBS News on-the-air team to explain what it all meant. I remember saying something pompous like this to Blair Clark, who replied, in a kind yet puzzled voice, "How on earth are you going to do that?" I told him I hadn't any idea but that I was sure it would cost a lot of money.

"Oh, dear," he said. "I was afraid you were going to say that."

Blair Clark left for other pastures long before the money spent by the three networks on convention and election coverage had burgeoned to a total of about $75 million in a presidential year.

Bill Eames, Bobby Wussler and I first turned our attention to the question of how we could collect the raw vote fast. We thought we might plant a few dozen or even a few hundred reporters around New York during a municipal election to supplement the AP, but the idea of doing something like that nationally slowed even Bobby, who liked operating on a small scale only if a grand scale was not immediately available. To stay competitive we made plans to collect the raw vote more quickly than the other networks by making arrangements with a few veteran news people in states where polls closed early, people who promised they could outperform the wire services. But essentially I knew there was not likely to be anything we could do in the realm of collecting and tabulating the votes that would go beyond keeping us more or less competitive. If we were to make a breakthrough, it had to be in some other fashion.

As luck would have it, pollster Lou Harris was a friend and neighbor of mine and of Fred Friendly's. He was also an ardent—and expert—political buff. I had known Lou since the early 1950s, when he was just striking out on his own. By 1960 he had become nationally known and was an advisor to Jack Kennedy both before and during the 1960 Democratic Convention in Los Angeles. I had been a floor reporter there, and Lou, acting in all good faith, had given me the kind of tip a reporter dreams about—although in this case the dream turned out to be a nightmare.

When Kennedy was nominated, the big question was his choice of a vice president. For twenty-four hours, I and every other reporter in Los Angeles dug for the answer. Harris kept insisting the choice hadn't been made. But hours later, on the convention floor, he nodded when I asked him if Kennedy had picked his running mate. "But I can't tell you, Bill," he said. "I just swore I wouldn't."

"Well, just tell me one thing, Lou. No, you don't even have to do that . . . There was a dope story this morning in one of the L.A. papers. It said, 'Symington to get veep nod.' Lou, if that's wrong, just shake your head."

Lou Harris looked at me and smiled. "Remember," he said, "I never said a word."

I went up to the anchor booth area as fast as I could and found Sig Mickelson, the CBS News chief. I didn't tell him my source—only that it was a damn good one, close to the Kennedys, and that they had picked Stuart Symington. A few seconds later I went into the anchor booth itself and sat next to Cronkite and told him and his loyal audience that the vice presidential choice had been made. Symington was the man. Walter said that, coming from Bill Leonard, the tip was good enough for him. When word came a few hours later of the last-minute deal that made Lyndon Johnson Kennedy's choice, I had made a fool of both of us. To their eternal credit, neither Mickelson nor Cronkite—nor anyone else at CBS News— ever held it against me. (Harris told me later, and others have confirmed it, that at the time he talked to me, Symington had indeed been the choice. A lot has been written about the strategy of offering the job to Johnson, apparently with the expectation that he would not take it.)

Lou was fascinated by my election unit assignment, and almost from the start of our first informal conversations about the job ahead, I knew that I needed him to help me—that his polling expertise might be just what CBS needed. At one point we talked about the IBM computers and the way they had been used in the last election. I asked Lou if he thought material could be developed from the computer that was reliable enough to be used for calling election results. Could we use computers seriously, not just as entertainment gimmicks, as we'd been using them?

"I think so," Lou said promptly. "If I can come up with a way to pick out just the right sample precincts *and* we could put people in those precincts to report their results back quickly *and* we can process the whole thing almost instantly through those IBM computers—why, we could call a particular election in almost no time at all once the polls have closed!"

"But Lou," I said, "isn't that what they've been doing with the computers on election nights?"

"Yes, and no," he answered. "There's a term among computer people: GIGO—garbage in, garbage out—and from what I've observed, they haven't spent too much effort making sure of their samples. And, of course, no one has taken the important step you're talking about, using it as a tool instead of a gimmick."

I asked Lou to go ahead and research the possibilities. He cautioned me it might be an expensive proposition, and he was certainly right about that. What Lou Harris came up with was the beginning of what we later named Vote Profile Analysis. After doing research in the field, Harris found a number of key precincts—perhaps forty or fifty per state—whose past voting patterns, when taken together, gave quite an accurate profile of the state as a whole. The methodology has changed considerably, and for the better, since those days, but it was Lou Harris, working with a couple of bright young men from IBM, who got it rolling.

It was not many months old before the election unit proved to be something more than its creators had bargained for. The graphic display on the old election set looked old-fashioned and the numbers were difficult to change. A project for modernization was as expensive as it was badly needed. Our plans to beef up raw vote collection added many more thousands of dollars not originally included in what had passed for an election-night budget.

I began to lobby Ernie Leiser, Blair Clark and Dick Salant about the vast potential of Vote Profile Analysis. It was difficult for Salant and his financial deputy, David Klinger, to understand why Lou Harris should be charging us $30,000 for each state for which he would provide VPA. That was a hell of a lot of money in those days, and the suspicion existed in some quarters that we were paying more than top dollar for an untested product. I recognized that we were taking a considerable financial risk, but one thing seemed most important of all to me: VPA might just prove to be the way we could call elections faster than ever before. And I wanted to get there first.

Left to my own foolish devices, I might have commissioned Lou Harris to prepare VPA estimates for more states than we ended up covering. As it was, a combination of factors, the most important of which might have been money, limited us to seven. That was probably just as well. For television audiences, the shock of network predictions, estimates, declarations of winners—call them what you will—took a lot of getting used to.

For years, whenever a viewer looked at the screen and saw figures such as

SMITH   1,536

JONES   987

it had meant that Smith was leading Jones in the early returns. What we were doing now, early in the game, through our analysis of sample precincts, was telling the viewer flat out who we estimated had won, regardless of who seemed to be "leading" in the votes counted. And if an election was going to end up too close for us to call, we would say that—even though the tabulated vote might show Smith well ahead of Jones.

There were thirteen races in the seven states to which we applied our new VPA methods in 1962, and we either called all of them correctly or properly labeled them too close to call. But the race I remember after all these years is the one in which Governor John B. Swainson was running for reelection in Michigan against a fellow named George Romney.

We had a remote feed direct to Swainson headquarters and we switched there and put him on the air moments after our sample precincts showed him to be defeated. He could not have been more surprised. In fact, it was obvious he did not believe us, for the popular vote tallies of all three networks showed that he was *ahead* of Romney. Furthermore, no other network and no local Michigan station had even suggested he had lost! But, based on the returns of those VPA precincts, our figures showed him a reasonably close though eventual loser.

We switched our cameras next to Romney and told him our predictions. He didn't believe us either. We stuck to our guns, and as the evening wore on and the tabulated vote totals from Michigan began to swell, the lead finally shifted to Romney. He won, but the race ended up uncomfortably close, and, not for the last time, I thought to myself: My God, what if we'd been wrong!

All in all, the 1962 election-night effort was a success. NBC still won the ratings rather handily, and they generally collected the raw vote a little faster. But VPA had accomplished just what we hoped it would. And it had given us a perfect dry run for the races that counted . . . the ones in 1964.

Quite overwhelming my small first election-unit success was a personal tragedy. It was in August 1962 that Kappy's older son, Peter Wallace, died in a freak mountain-climbing accident in Greece. He was nineteen, about to start his junior year at Yale, already a writer of exceptional promise—a boy who combined sweetness of personality with such a high order of eagerness and determination that somehow one felt he was sure to make his mark in the world.

A quarter of a century later, I still find his death hard to believe, and even harder to understand. Peter is buried in Greece on the mountainside where he fell, which looks out over the shimmering bay of Corinth and the quiet countryside of that great and ancient civilization he had come to explore.

After our good start in '62, the election unit began gearing up for what would turn out to be the single busiest year of my life, 1964. We had to plan for and produce two separate weeks of gavel-to-gavel convention coverage—on opposite coasts. There were half a dozen presidential primaries to be covered, beginning with New Hampshire in mid-winter and ending with California in June. And once all that was out of the way, there would be election night itself. It promised to be twice as competitive and four times as expensive as the '62 election.

If I had been a more experienced executive, I would have realized that we were trying to do too much with too little. Wussler, Eames and I spent half our lives on planes. On the ground we were stretched much too thin and were constantly shifting gears. One day Wussler and I might be in San Francisco trying to close deals for hotels at the GOP convention nearly a year down the road. Next, getting off the red-eye back in New York, I'd barely make it to a meeting to fight for enough money to provide VPA coverage of *all* the continental states—a far cry from the first efforts of '62—before leaving just in time to catch a charter to Atlantic City, where the Democratic Convention would be held. Thaler, Eames, Wussler and I were all busy to the point of endangering our health.

Once during those hectic times I mentioned to Eames that I hadn't seen Wussler for a couple of days. "Hey, you're right," he said, "neither have I." Wussler traveled far and fast, but it wasn't like him not to call in once or twice a day. His secretary thought he was in Oregon, but she wasn't sure. She began making calls. Bobby was finally located in a hospital somewhere in Portland, suffering from what was at first diagnosed as a possible heart attack but was then downgraded to simple exhaustion. Forty-eight hours later Bobby was back on his feet, working those eighteen-hour days again with the rest of us.

The New Hampshire primary was our first big test in 1964, and VPA came through again. Lou Harris had some trepidation about applying VPA sampling techniques to primaries, but he thought he had things worked out. At any rate, only a few minutes after the polls had closed in most areas of the state, our figures showed that Henry Cabot Lodge had won, very much of an upset. We went on the air and called the race well ahead of the other networks: Lodge wins the primary. VPA was still batting a thousand.

To date, 1964 had been a wild enough time for me; the frenetic pace simply accelerated when a major change in CBS News management took place almost on the eve of the New Hampshire primary. Dick Salant was dismissed as President and brought back to man a useless post at corporate headquarters. His unpardonable sin? The Cronkite news ratings were not up to the Huntley-Brinkley figures, and sinking news ratings were something Paley could not abide.

I was genuinely sorry to see Dick go. He loved the news business, heart and soul, and it seemed the whole organization had just begun to get to know him. He governed quietly; perhaps too much so. Years later, I asked Bill Paley what he'd had in mind when he removed Salant. "I thought the place needed shaking up," he said, "and maybe Friendly could do it." It certainly didn't take long before everyone was aware of CBS News' new boss: Fred W. Friendly.

Fred and I, of course, were friends, but close as we had been during my *CBS Reports* days, I had scarcely seen him for more than two years. With all the other burdens I was shouldering in 1964, I hardly needed an intensely curious, wildly energetic new boss who was totally ignorant of what we were doing, although, in the long run, he would be responsible for how well our election-year coverage turned out. It took no soothsayer to predict that our performance in 1964 would affect CBS News' standing for years to come.

And so, lashed now not only by the competition but by Friendly as well, we scrapped our way from primary to primary. New Hampshire, Indiana, Oregon, finally California. In Oregon each network had stationed reporters in nearly every state precinct to count the raw vote quickly. It was NBC News that called the results first, a few minutes ahead of us—much to our surprise. It was bound to happen, but in Oregon we fully realized for the first time that two could play this game.

We hardly had the time to feel sorry for ourselves. The California primary, pitting Barry Goldwater against Nelson Rockefeller, was just down the coast and the calendar.

We were moving so fast, and under such pressure, that one day Bobby Wussler came to me in New York clutching several sheets of paper covered with what looked like a computer printout.

"Hey, boss," he said, "look what I just found in my desk. A bill from the Oregon telephone company for $36,000 for phones we installed in all those precincts for the primary. I threw it in there three months ago and forgot all about it!"

"Well," I said, "you better hurry up and get it paid before they turn off all those thousands of unmanned phones out there."

Goldwater and Rockefeller threw everything they had into the California primary, which was widely perceived as critical to the nomination. All three networks, in an absolute frenzy of vote-counting preparation, made arrangements to station people at virtually every one of California's 32,861 precincts, from which they would phone in totals. That meant a total of nearly 100,000 employees—some paid, some volunteers. Thousands of dollars were spent on special phone installations and many more thousands on statewide long-distance phone calls. All this in search of the brief victory of momentarily posting a slightly larger total of votes than the rival networks during one special election broadcast madness.

There was high interest in the California primary, and the timing of the poll closing (10:00 P.M. on the East Coast, 9:00 in the Midwest) fell nicely into prime time. Rockefeller had been leading comfortably in the pre-primary polls, but over the weekend before the June 2 election, news broke that his wife, Happy, had given birth to a baby. This provided a sharp reminder to California voters that, not long before, Rockefeller had divorced his wife of many years to marry a younger woman, and last-minute polling by Lou Harris showed the race to be narrowing suddenly.

Walter Cronkite was at the anchor desk that night, as usual, and Fred Friendly had flown out from New York. Our headquarters studio in the Los Angeles Biltmore was ablaze with all the paraphernalia of a very big broadcast indeed. The "vote war" among the networks had in itself become big news, and at one point I complained to one of our press people that there seemed to be more reporters covering our reporters than there were our reporters covering the political developments.

With the closing of the polls in California, the television action started almost immediately. Our early vote totals were not very different from those offered by the other networks: All showed Rockefeller with a small but apparently significant lead when Lou Harris consulted me shortly after seven o'clock Pacific time. We bent over an IBM computer printout. "Now look at this," he hissed. "I think we've got a call. It's Goldwater!"

The figures amassed from our VPA precincts around the state showed that Goldwater would win with 51.6 percent of the vote, just above our margin-for-error guidelines. I fired a series of questions at Harris. Were there still figures to come in from some VPA precincts? Yes, but not enough of them to change things. How could we have a fair sample of the state when none of the VPA precincts in the Bay area could have reported in?

"Don't worry about that," he said. "We interviewed people coming out of polling places in our sample precincts up there and they'll do okay as substitutes for the actual VPA precincts. Not to worry." As far as I know, this was the first time exit polling was ever used to assist in election projections.

Lou Harris and I and a small body of our computer and polling experts checked and rechecked the figures. As a few more key precincts came in, the clear indication of a narrow Goldwater victory held firm.

It was 7:15 P.M. I turned to Harris. "I want to be one hundred percent sure."

"We're within our guidelines," said Lou. (We had set guidelines below which our VPA estimate could not fall before using the projection to say that a candidate had won the race. If the sample precincts fell below the guideline, we announced that the race was too close to call. The Goldwater figures were above the guideline level, although not by much.)

I told Friendly I was about to call the race for Goldwater. He glanced over at the tabulated totals that showed Rockefeller in the lead.

"Is it close?" he asked.

I told him most of the VPA precincts were in, and that we were within our guidelines, holding steady.

"Well," he said, "it's up to you."

At 7:21 P.M. Walter Cronkite, hardly able to keep the astonishment out of his voice, announced to the nation that CBS News estimated Barry Goldwater would be the winner. Neither of the other networks followed with confirming estimates—not in the next few minutes, the next half hour, or indeed in the next several hours.

Thus began, barring one or two evenings off Anzio, the longest night of my life. Much that followed seemed to point toward our having made a wrong call. As the last VPA precincts reported in, our final estimate of the race—while still showing Goldwater the winner—was actually below the guideline figure, which meant that had we had that figure early in the evening I would never have made the call, nor indeed would Lou Harris have recommended it.

As the tabulated votes flooded in, Rockefeller looked like a winner. He was well ahead. The other networks, although claiming the race was too close to call on the basis of their estimates, couldn't help looking at that vote board and reflecting on how well Rockefeller appeared to be doing.

All through the evening I continued to whistle in what I hoped was not the dark. I kept assuring Friendly he didn't have a damn thing to worry about. I knew he had a meeting in New York the next morning and wanted to catch the red-eye, and I told him he could go without a worry in the world about the California primary. He looked a little doubtful as he left for the airport.

Fred loves to tell the story of that plane ride.

"When I got on the plane, I told the stewardess I was going to try to get a little sleep and asked her if the pilot could let me know if he heard anything about the result of the California primary. I was dead to the world, and the next thing I heard was the pilot's voice over the PA. 'Good morning, ladies and gentlemen. We're just about to make our approach into the New York City area, and it's going to be a beautiful day. If you look out of the right side of the aircraft, you can just see the island of Manhattan rising out of the early morning mist, almost like a painting. And by the way, if you're interested, Governor Rockefeller has won the California primary.' The last fifteen minutes of that flight seemed to take forever. I got to a phone and I called you, Bill, and the most reassuring thing I ever heard was you saying, 'What the hell did you wake me for, Fred? I told you not to worry.'"

In the six or seven hours since Fred's departure, a lot had happened. The networks' huge vote-collection apparatus had amassed nearly all the raw vote and just about confirmed the Goldwater victory. What had confused matters was the wire services: They were hopelessly behind the networks in vote collection, to say nothing of lacking a scientific method of estimating the outcome of the race. With what little raw vote it had collected, the AP came to the conclusion that Rockefeller had won. This news went across the country as gospel, even being carried on the CBS flagship station in New York, only hours after it had carried our network broadcast the night before, signaling the Goldwater victory. It confused the hell out of everybody and shamed the wire services when they woke up to what really had happened, and how dreadfully they had been outmanned.

Our very early Goldwater call in California turned out to be a pyrrhic victory at best. Goldwater's final margin was so slight it was apparent that calling the race early had meant we might have been more lucky than smart. A small storm of criticism broke around Lou Harris and me, some of it in the press, some from Stanton and Paley. For a couple of precious weeks, when I might have been better employed getting ready for the Republican convention looming just ahead, I was kept very busy defending myself for not having been more cautious, for not having better guidelines—for just about everything except not electing Rockefeller. As a result, we tightened the guidelines and made some other changes to improve the VPA process, which to that point, however, had never called a race inaccurately.

In the midst of all the instant replays and the second guessing I said to Bobby Wussler, "Winning is awful! But suppose we had lost?"

Bobby smiled. "You'd be back doing local radio."

The California primary signaled the end of the absurd competition among the major networks to collect votes. Only a few days later, representatives of AP, UPI, ABC News, CBS News and NBC News met and began to work out the agreement that led to the creation of the News Election Service, an independent organization that collects vote information and distributes it to the networks. With reluctant Justice Department approval of this arrangement not to compete to collect the vote, the great vote war of 1964 came to an end.

The GOP Convention provided me with my next opportunity to wade deep into a sea of trouble, and I was up to the challenge. We had worked hard getting ready for it; at great expense we'd built a huge booth overlooking the hall, with control and directing facilities right next to it, hoping they would provide a sense of unity among all of us who were programming, broadcasting and directing the coverage. We had carefully selected a floor reporting team (including Dan Rather, Mike Wallace, Roger Mudd and Martin Agronsky) to compete with NBC's crack people: Sander Vanocur, Frank McGee and company. A review of the tapes of the 1960 coverage convinced us CBS had probably spent too much time with Cronkite handling the coverage alone in the anchor booth. NBC not only took its cameras to the lively convention floor more often, but in the booth it had the advantage of two newscasters batting things back and forth.

Under normal circumstances, the CBS News staff would have been resentful of outsiders giving them a hand with political coverage. There was one exception: At the suggestion of Blair Clark, I managed to make a very informal arrangement with Theodore H. White to be a part of our coverage team. Teddy was on the campaign trail, as hot and heavy as any candidate, gathering material for his book *The Making of the President—1964*. Along with Lou Harris, he would brief our people on the day before a primary or on election night. He was wonderful at it, perceptive and enthusiastic, Teddy never sneered, never was bored, loved every minute of a process that turns off many a smart reporter. In general, the more sensitive the writer, the less buoyant his spirit. Not so with Teddy. He'd burst into town, join the gang, and ask joyously, "Where are the parties?" With it all, a Pulitzer Prize awaited him down the next bend. The campaign trails will never be the same without Teddy White. No one will ever love them so much.

By the time the Republican Convention rolled around, my relationship with Walter Cronkite had, quite naturally, changed. Already Bill Eames, Wussler and I were charter members of the CAFOC—Care and Feeding of Cronkite—Club. We met daily, sometimes late at night. The trick was to get Walter to do what *we* wanted him to do and thought was good for the broadcast or the news division—and to keep him reasonably happy in the process. *His* trick was generally to resist suggestions that involved change. Walter was, by nature, a tad suspicious, skeptical of people who professed to do things for his own good, particularly if it might alter his role in the proceedings and even more particularly if it threatened to reduce his role.

Brought up in the old UPI election mold, where a vote tallied was a vote tallied, Walter had the devil's own time embracing VPA projections. He had gotten used to Dick Salant and his low-key approach, but Friendly was a different matter. Fred was into everything, and that made Walter nervous. Then there was Bill Leonard. Leonard was beginning to get him nervous too. *He* was into every last thing! Well, he supposed it was all part of Bill's job. But why didn't they just let him cover things the way he always had? After all, he was the only one who had it all in his head, who knew what was going on.

That was the problem. The ratings showed that Walter, good as he was, couldn't hold an audience hour after hour, particularly during a convention that lacked much action or suspense. Friendly felt that it would be of some help to inject frequent doses of Eric

Sevareid into things, as a more reflective sort of "Brinkley." We gave some thought to seating Eric next to Walter so that he might turn to him for occasional observations, although an actual coanchor was never contemplated. Our musings quickly became academic. The minute I began to talk about a place for Eric in the anchor booth area, Walter exploded. In the end, we found a place for Sevareid that Walter considered only mildly threatening, but we'd been off to a bad start.

The 1964 Republican Convention will probably be remembered for its display of the first wave of conservative unity that later grew into the Reagan tide. No one who was there will forget the roar of hatred that greeted Nelson Rockefeller when he tried to have his say. Even Lyndon Johnson would have received a far better reception from the GOP.

Our coverage of the convention went poorly. Our plan had been to have our cameras go to our floor reporters early and often, for Walter to act more as a quarterback and less as the player who carried the ball most of the time. Easier said than done.

Through our director, Don Hewitt, I would ask Walter every now and then to hand things over to one of the floor reporters. As often as not, he'd keep talking. It finally became more and more obvious that he was digging in his heels. At one point, when he was off the air, I went into his anchor booth, smoking mad, and told him that when he got an order to switch to the floor I expected him to carry it out. At another point, Walter actually stomped out of the booth for a few minutes. By the end of the convention, things were going a bit more smoothly—and all through it our floor reporters had performed very well—but it was too late. The ratings came out day after day, one as bad as another: NBC had beaten us handily every single day.

Even with the benefit of hindsight, I very much doubt if anything could have been done to reverse that. We had blown it. Even the most casual observer could see that our coverage had been slow and boring. It was painfully obvious that some of the conflict going on behind the scenes had come through on the air.

One of the strengths of the election unit had been my good relationship with the most important person at CBS News, Walter Cronkite, and somehow in the pressure cooker of the campaign year that relationship had suffered. I didn't think so at the time, but from the perspective of years, I can say that a great deal of the fault for this was mine. In 1964 I was neither an experienced nor a sensitive executive, merely an energetic one. My only training in supervising people had come in the U.S. Navy under wartime conditions, when an order was an order. It was absurd for me to have acted as if Cronkite were part of a ship's complement of which I was the commanding officer. Cronkite was Cronkite, and in the heat of the convention I should have remembered the aims of our CAFOC Club. Somehow I should have found a way to get the best out of him instead of the worst.

Abject self-recrimination was not, however, in the forefront of my mind when Friendly and I were called over to see Paley and Stanton as soon as the convention was over and they had had time to absorb the dismal ratings and indifferent reviews. Paley, obviously very upset, knew that a great deal of money had been spent in the convention effort—enough to bring forth bitter complaints from some television network people who resented not only the money we siphoned from them, but the considerable amount of air time the convention coverage took from regular, and profitable, programming. Paley always wanted to eat his cake and have it too—and who can blame him? He liked to perform public service (and reap credit for it) with one hand, and turn a large profit with the other. Here we stood: the new President of CBS News and the head of his expensive new election unit, their first major effort a resounding failure.

The first question, as I recall, came not from Paley but from Frank Stanton. "What the hell happened to Walter?"

"Walter wasn't quite himself," Friendly offered weakly.

"Why not?" snapped Paley. "Was he sick?"

"No," I said, "I don't think so."

"Well," said the Chairman, "I thought the idea was that Walter was going to do a little less, and you were going to spread the load around, so the pace would pick up. Wasn't that the idea, didn't you tell me that's what you all had in mind, Fred?"

Fred looked at me, as if to say, You tell 'em.

"Well, sir, that *was* the idea but Walter sort of . . . I guess you could say . . . resisted it."

"What does that mean?"

"I would, for instance, pass the word to go to the floor—perhaps we had an interview lined up and the timing on those things can be tricky, you can't hold those guys still forever—and Walter would delay sometimes and not pay attention to Don Hewitt, so that tended to throw things off."

The Chairman's voice rose perilously. "You mean he would get what amounted to an *order* and he wouldn't obey it?! Is that what would happen? Did you actually give him *orders* and he wouldn't carry them *out*?"

I realized we were sinking fast.

"I wouldn't put it quite that way," Fred interposed. "You know, Walter is Walter."

"I don't know anything about 'Walter is Walter,'" snapped the Chairman. "It sounds to me as if Walter wouldn't do what he was told, and *you* weren't able to do anything about it!" Paley had hit the nail on the head.

Friendly and I fell silent, praying that his outburst might put an end to the matter.

It was just the beginning.

"Who do you think could replace Walter?" Paley asked a few minutes later.

Fred and I looked at each other in astonishment. I think Stanton too may have been as surprised as we were.

"Do you mean at a convention?" I mumbled. "Well, I suppose down the line a few years . . . probably Roger Mudd."

"I don't mean down the line, I mean right now. We can't have people who won't take orders, and anyway it's not working. What about right now?"

Almost immediately, Fred and I fell over each other's words. We both said we thought it would be disruptive to make a change between the two conventions. But the Chairman had the bit in his teeth. I added that if a change were to be made right now, there was no one at CBS News who could fill Cronkite's shoes.

By the time the meeting ended, we had come up with the names of Bob Trout and Roger Mudd as potential coanchors. And Friendly had promised Paley and Stanton that he would give the idea serious consideration and, from the point of view of the news division, recommend either for or against them.

As far as I know, Fred actually consulted only one other person about the idea: Ernie Leiser, producer of the *Evening News*. Leiser was shocked. When Friendly went across town a day or two later to report back to the Chairman, he carried the unanimous recommendation of the men at the top of the news division not to oust Cronkite. Certain that it would be accepted, I was astonished when Fred announced to us that he must replace Walter for next month's Democratic Convention in Atlantic City, and that Trout and Mudd had been named coanchors.

The next day Fred and I flew out to California, met Walter in an airport lounge and broke the news to him. He took it like the gentleman he is.

The removal of Cronkite hurt only CBS News. Trout and Mudd did their best, but people watched NBC anyway—perhaps even more so out of sympathy for Walter.

Exhausted and discouraged, I faced the last task of what our sparklingly original self-promotion was calling Campaign '64. The election unit's promising first efforts had made hardly a dent in the dominance of the NBC News ratings. CBS News was badly shaken by the Cronkite replacement: As far as the troops were concerned, the unpopular decision had been Friendly's and mine—nor did we suggest anything else to Walter, though he may have guessed where it originated. I had little time to brood, in any case. Ahead lay the election campaign, with a series of attendant special broadcasts, and then election night itself.

Lyndon Johnson was a heavy favorite against Barry Goldwater. Once again, we were staking a great deal on our ability to call races early. Extending this technique to every state instead of just a few meant increasing the risk of confusing viewers. They might see a tabulated vote in which Goldwater, perhaps, or a particular senator, was apparently leading in a particular state, while at the same time their screens might display a check mark indicating that Johnson, or the senator's opponent, had in fact won the race. We spent hours working out the appropriate language to make the returns clear and understandable to the viewer, but I must admit sometimes even our own correspondents got mixed up. It was literally years before that language began to sound more or less natural—and comprehensible. But neither CBS nor the other networks won friends for doing one of the things journalists are supposed to do: get the news to the people as quickly as possible.

A few days after the 1964 election night during which Lyndon Johnson was declared winner even before the polls had closed in California, an angry postcard addressed to CBS found its way to my desk. "You *bastards!*" it read. "Election night used to be fun. You spoiled it with your goddamned gimmicks."

The author of this message spoke for any number of viewers who in years past had settled down to their TV, or their radio, and relished the suspense as stations, networks, wire services and newspapers, more or less cooperating with election authorities scattered over three thousand counties, gradually discerned how the nation had voted at the polls hours earlier. As the saying goes, getting there is half the fun. Somehow, though, the networks' flat, swift assertions that X would be the next President or the next Senator took something away from the election process, just as jet air travel took away some of the charm of leisurely trips on ocean liners.

The postcard had reached the right man. If blame is the correct word, I deserve a fair share of it for taking the fun out of election-night TV viewing. I offer myself up willingly because elections were so obviously not created for audience amusement; as we became more sophisticated in election reporting, entertainment suffered at the expense of information delivered.

Our first major decision concerning the 1964 election night had to do with who the broadcast anchor should be. As I recall, Friendly, Leiser and I arrived at it in about five seconds: Cronkite—if he would do it in the wake of the trauma of the conventions.

Walter said yes, he would be glad to take the job, and things were back almost the way they had been in the old days. We had a superb supporting team—Harry Reasoner, Roger Mudd, Dan Rather, Eric Sevareid, Mike Wallace, Charles Collingwood and many others.

To this day, I couldn't tell you why that particular evening went so well for CBS News. It was not an exciting election: Johnson won by a landslide. And CBS, too, apparently. Jack Gould of *The New York Times*, an enormously influential and highly regarded television critic who was not given to hyperbole, provided a review of the network's election-night coverage that was all the tonic we needed:

CBS BY A LANDSLIDE!
Network's Coverage of the Election Is Called Far Superior to Its Rivals

The Columbia Broadcasting System turned in a superb journalistic beat last night, running away with the major honors in reporting President Johnson's election victory.

In clarity of presentation the network led all the way, and in speed it was way up front for at least an hour and a half. In a medium where time is of the essence, the performance of CBS was of landslide proportions . . .

Gould's review rolled on. Those comments went a long way toward erasing the trauma of NBC's rating wipe-out at the conventions and the disruption caused by the replacement of Cronkite at Atlantic City. And, of course, they underscored our faith in the vote projection system that we had developed. As far as my own career was concerned, CBS's election-night coverage was obviously of value. But most important of all was the effect it had on the entire CBS News organization. We were the best. We knew it. *The New York Times* confirmed it.

A word about the famous—or infamous—1968 Democratic Convention in Chicago, the one that resulted almost literally in a war between Mayor Daley and the Chicago police force on the one hand and thousands of demonstrators on the other. Daley was bent on order, the demonstrators on disorder. In the process of keeping the peace, Daley won the battle but lost the war. Chicago lost it as well. Daley did his best to keep newsmen from covering the troubles around Grant Park, and he actually succeeded in keeping us from most live coverage through a series of arbitrary obstructionist regulations. But sooner or later all America saw, live or tape-delayed, cops beating people, cops bullying and bruising unarmed men and women. That sorry image remains in the national memory.

From the point of view of newsmen, the 1968 convention was totally frustrating. We were "live" in a convention hall where there was a lot of security but not much of a story. Bobby Kennedy was dead; the nomination of Hubert Humphrey was a foregone conclusion. The real story was out there on the streets of Chicago, and we were forced to jackhammer into our live broadcast from the hall bits and pieces of it as tape and film filtered in, twenty minutes, forty minutes, an hour or more after the event.

A single emotion was abroad in Chicago. Anger. Anger over Vietnam. Over Bobby. Over Martin Luther King, Jr. Mayor Daley and all his men were angry. It was their Chicago, and it had been invaded. And of course all the men and women from all the networks and local stations who had come to Chicago to tell a story were angry. Everyone was angry. I remember thinking, as we left town after that tense and, to some of our people, very dangerous week, "Well, at least we got out of here alive." Not only demonstrators and police but more than a few newsmen had bruises to show for the ugly confrontations that took place on Chicago's streets and in its parks. There was palpable tension inside the convention hall, too. Mike Wallace was detained by the police after a scuffle on the floor. Walter Cronkite had an exclusive but oddly "soft" interview with the embattled Mayor Daley. No one can point with a great deal of pride to Chicago, summer of '68.

For many years I continued to have responsibility for the CBS News election and convention coverage, although after 1964, the election unit itself was ably run by others, notably Bobby Wussler, Bob Chandler, Warren Mitofsky and most recently Joan Richman. We developed in-house capability to do the things that Lou Harris had done for us in the early days. Competition among the three networks did not slacken much, if at all, in the election-night game, and ABC News increasingly made its presence felt in political coverage as well as in general.

The costs of political coverage continued to escalate, very roughly doubling every four years, and the proliferation of primaries made coverage even more expensive. With each election year, all three networks began to make increasing use of so-called exit polls—informal canvassing of voters just after they had left their precinct on election day. At first, exit polling was not used, at least by CBS News, to call a race, but a combination of improved polling techniques and the networks' escalating competition got us all into that business, too.

Today, the networks seem to have slowed down—finally—in one aspect of what became political coverage overkill: Gavel-to-gavel convention coverage is virtually a thing of the past.

It was not always so: The tradition of complete television coverage began in 1952 with two thrilling conventions, exciting almost from beginning to end, and a new medium flexing its muscles and performing a major public service for the first time. No one questioned, when 1956 rolled around, whether we would all do it again, gavel to gavel and even beyond. The policy of NBC News was to stay on longer than CBS; sometimes at conventions CBS would upstage NBC by starting its coverage earlier. Back and forth, early and late, the competing networks disrupted regular program scheduling so thoroughly it did not make much difference how long any of us stayed on. Correspondents rehashed the night's doings until they were nearly hoarse and until only the sturdiest political buffs were still with them.

Walter Cronkite used to say, in defense of gavel-to-gavel coverage, that America could use a good civics lesson once every four years. I always had trouble believing that so much force-feeding was very effective, and the facts bore out my feeling: During convention weeks, people by the millions sought out independent stations and watched reruns of old-time movie favorites rather than tuning in on the interminable political coverage offered by the major networks. But most people within a news division have their own special perspective. The conventions, and indeed the whole Presidential political year, represent the best opportunity to test the troops in action, so to speak. It is the time when we find out what our people are really made of—technicians, correspondents, producers, even vice presidents. Ultimately, it was this same rigorous and extensive training at the conventions that gave network television people the power to rise, technically and editorially, to the sad occasion of the Kennedy assassination with superb coverage over four dark days.

Election coverage in the future is sure to come in for some tough scrutiny by network officials. Common sense dictates that it is hardly a wise financial choice to support an elaborate three-tiered system of vote gathering and estimating (the News Election Service, special precincts, exit polling) whose rewards are here today and gone tomorrow.

Over the years, the enormous prestige a network news division gained from "winning" the war for the best convention, primary or election-night coverage, either through ratings or reviews or a combination of both, has dissipated to a considerable extent. Increasingly, reputations are made—or lost—by the performance of news teams in some national or international crisis.

Certainly we will never again see the likes of those wild and woolly days of the '64 Presidential primary, when armies of network reporters fanned out over every nook and cranny of the largest state in the Union.

Amen.

7

THE
EXECUTIVE
TRAP

———

How did I ever get myself into the executive trap? I must say I saw it coming, for long before the end of the frantic campaign year of 1964 Fred Friendly had made it clear that my days as a producer and correspondent were numbered.

"I can't run this place without you," he'd moan seductively.

And so, in January 1965 I found myself a vice president of CBS News. Like all red-blooded news people, I despised vice presidents on sight. It was the principle of the thing: There they were in the CBS directory, hundreds of them. Thick as flies. Buzzing around to no purpose.

The people at CBS News sometimes ate at a little French restaurant on 57th Street called Biarritz. Correspondent Hughes Rudd, mighty gifted at his best, mighty wicked under lubrication, was there one day enjoying a liquid lunch. He spotted me at a nearby table and hurried over.

"You used to *do* something!" he shouted. "Now you don't *do* anything. Why don't you *do* something?"

"You're right, Hughes," I said. "I don't do a goddamned thing. Our little secret."

He shook his head sadly, as if to say, Another poor son of a bitch gone down the tube, and drifted back to his seat.

Although I had finally become an executive almost by accident— just as haphazardly, it seems, as I had become "talent" some twenty years earlier—I never regretted the fact. In keeping with company policy, no CBS executive, from Chairman Paley on down, receives screen credit for his efforts. But there were plenty of other compensations. I found that helping to run CBS News, to shape its product and policies, to be in the heart of all its action was fulfilling indeed.

Unlike Gaul, with its three parts, all news is divided into two divisions: "hard" and "soft." Hard news is what's happening today; soft news is what takes longer, the documentaries, the specials that are not "instant." Soft news, said Friendly, would be my province. I balked.

Except for my *CBS Reports* days, all my working life had been spent dealing with the business of today's story today, tomorrow's story tomorrow. If I was going to be pulled out of the so-called creative ranks and moved to the front office, I would have much preferred the hard-news side of the business, and I told Fred so.

Fred responded that because of my experience, the election unit would continue to report to me, albeit under a new executive producer. This pleased me; the conventions and elections took a lot of planning, to be sure, but once under way they were hard news— they provided fast-moving high drama, my kind of story.

Still, I wanted to deal with the news every day, not once every two or four years. But Friendly was not to be deterred from assigning me to soft news. He had more than one reason for pushing me in that direction, not the least of which was that the wounds of the 1964 convention were not yet healed. Perhaps a more compelling reason was that the *Evening News* lagged in ratings behind Huntley-Brinkley and a fresh, dynamic approach in hard-news coverage might help. For that, why not turn to sources outside of CBS News, to the best of print journalism? After considering several candidates, including Abe Rosenthal of *The New York Times*, Fred finally chose Gordon Manning of *Newsweek* to be Vice President of News. Fred also knew that, with the whole shop to worry about now, he himself would not have as much time to nurse his beloved documentaries; he needed someone he knew well who knew about documentaries to look after them.

Fred was understandably nervous, and just a little uneasy, in the hard-news arena, where he was long on instinct but a little short on experience. As in everything, he wanted desperately, perhaps on occasions too desperately, to succeed. Few outside the forty-ninth state still remember the Alaska earthquake of 1964, but it was a sizable one, and a competitive news story at the time. CBS News was badly beaten on the story, and Fred was heard to moan, "This is my Bay of Pigs!" The word quickly got around the news organization that Fred Friendly really cared.

I took the job he offered. I had crossed over to the executive side: I was now Vice President of Programming.

Gordon Manning knew nothing about television. But he knew about news, and he cared about it. To Gordon story ideas were what life was all about. They flew from his typewriter—five, ten, twenty a day. Some were good, some weren't, but always they were charged with Gordon's driving enthusiasm. Why don't we? Could we? What if we? Did we ever? Why not? For a long time Gordon was too hesitant about his grasp of the medium to *insist* on things, but he was a quick study, and as the years rolled by he became wise in the ways of television, just as GI draftees in 1942 came to be battle-hardened by the war's end.

Gordon's head was directly connected to his fingertips. Armed with scraps of clippings or penciled notes he had scribbled to himself at home or somewhere over a drink, he would let loose what sometimes seemed like an endless barrage of little communiqués, his magic fingers beating to near death the poor typewriter at his elbow. Manning-grams became famous among news executives, producers and even correspondents, to whom he was careful and considerate in dropping notes of praise.

Helping to run CBS News under Friendly and Salant presented no end of tense and trying moments for me, though it was no particular fault of theirs. Working with Manning made things a comparative pleasure. He had a rollicking sense of humor and a supply of jokes that went back to the time he'd been a sports reporter in Boston. Gordon loved to tell about his interviews with Ted Williams. "He had the greatest eyes in the world, and I would say, 'Ted, what did that ball look like when a real fastball pitcher, like, say, a Bob Feller, threw one down the middle at you?' and Ted would hesitate a second and he would say, 'Gordon, it looked like a fucking watermelon.'"

Like so many of us, Gordon first fell in love with the news business generally, and later with CBS News specifically. Once bitten he was a passionate CBS News advocate.

CBS News was a special case among the CBS divisions. Although its only two customers were the CBS Radio and Television Networks, no line of authority extended from them to News, and quite properly so. In 1965 Fred Friendly's boss was Frank Stanton, whose interest in the health of the News division was palpable, as indeed was Paley's; I had come to realize that as head of the election unit. Now Manning and I joined Fred every week for a Paley-Stanton luncheon "across town," as we would call it, from our West 57th Street epicenter.

I remember that the tone of these luncheons was mildly defensive. What the Chairman's reaction might be to whatever we were about to propose, or what his feelings were about something he'd seen on the screen in the past day or two was anyone's guess. All three of us from 57th Street were rookies at the game of handling Paley, and it was both unnerving and instructive to observe the world's greatest expert at the art, Frank Stanton, display some trace of nervousness as one after the other of us botched things up.

Paley's news judgment was erratic, sometimes brilliant, occasionally a bit off course by our standards. On the occasion of Pope Paul VI's visit to New York City for instance—the first time a pontiff had ever set foot on American soil—Manning described with enthusiasm how we planned to cover every inch of his ride, from the airport into Manhattan and to the Mass he would conduct at Yankee Stadium, at a cost of many thousands of dollars and several hours of preemptive air time.

Paley seemed astonished that we planned any such elaborate coverage. "What for?" he kept saying. "How many people do you think care?"

"Mr. Paley," replied Gordon, patiently, "He's the *Pope.*"

"Well," said the Chairman, with irrefutable logic, "would you do that much if it was the head of the Episcopal church, or the biggest Jewish rabbi coming in from the airport? No. Then is it *fair* to do it for one religion? Is it *fair* from a CBS standpoint?"

If I remember, it was Frank Stanton who saved the day. Weren't the news people trying to say the Pope was a special, world-renowned personality, someone who in a sense was more than simply the head of a religion? The Chairman, not quite sure enough of his ground on this occasion to put his foot down, yielded. We covered the Pope's visit handsomely, but the thought that in the interest of *fairness* we might have had to toss it off as just another celebrity arrival from Europe stayed with us all for quite a while.

Much of the CBS building at 51 West 52 bears Frank Stanton's stamp, but Bill Paley personally tried to ensure that the restaurant at street level, The Ground Floor, was up to his high gourmet standards.

On the day before one of our luncheon meetings, Friendly, Manning and I decided we had better eat in the restaurant in case Paley grilled us about it. The food was atrocious, the service almost nonexistent and the prices sky-high. Friendly was so sick that night from the fish he had eaten that he could barely crawl to the office the next morning.

The Chairman was in a jolly mood during our working lunch

and, right on cue, as the dishes were being cleared away in the private dining room (where the food is *always* good), he asked, "Any of you fellows eaten at The Ground Floor yet?" The columns had been full of items about how closely William S. Paley was supervising the fare at The Ground Floor. That should have been enough warning for any sane employee. Friendly responded with what passed for a smile. Manning happened to be looking out the window. But Leonard, an admirer of the Chairman as trencherman supreme, spoke up, unabashed.

"Yes, sir."

"Well, what about it? You know food, William." A glance at Leonard's ample waistline. "Give us the truth now. No nonsense."

The blood drained from Stanton's face, as if he sensed I was just the kind of damn fool who'd take the Chairman literally.

Friendly eyed the ceiling. I was quiet for a moment, noting the warning signs. But the Chairman would want to hear the truth. Wouldn't he?

"We all had lunch there yesterday," I began. "Fred got sick from the fish. The service was really poor. And it was very expensive. Very."

The Chairman glared at me. "I see." He looked at his watch. "I guess that's it for today."

Later in the day Stanton called Friendly. "Keep Leonard away from Paley where food is concerned, or you fellows are going to have your hands full."

Anecdotes of this nature might suggest that people in the news division who dealt with Paley considered him a handful, and that is true enough. So did everyone with whom he came into contact. But his devotion to news, his sense of the importance of CBS's role in informing the public and doing so fairly and without favor has never been questioned. When I tangled with Paley over documentaries (I did very occasionally), it was always because he feared that our people had not played fair. When all is said and done, we must remember that CBS News would not have existed without William S. Paley or flourished without his support over fifty years.

Nevertheless, I had not been in my new job very long before I felt the sting of his wrath. The program in question, "The Berkeley Rebels," produced by Arthur Barron and broadcast in June 1965, was an innovative, touching and compassionate look at the untamed, rebellious youth of the times, especially those on the Berkeley campus. Arthur Barron was an extremely gifted filmmaker. The material he brought back from the field moved and flowed. It was alive. His scenes seemed to be the scenes that, as a producer, I always hoped to get but never did. Yet when I first viewed "The Berkeley Rebels" in rough cut, I bristled at the liberties Barron seemed to have taken. Certain scenes were so intimate that one couldn't help pondering whether they had been "directed," rather than simply "covered."

I didn't want to squeeze the life out of Barron's documentary—or anyone else's. But I had to explain to him, difficult though it was, that a precious hour of prime time was not there for him to "sell" his point of view, packaged and edited as if it were a commercial. CBS News, I had to say, tells the story, gives the facts, paints the picture as vividly, as truthfully and, above all, as *fairly* as possible. Then it must leave the public to come to its own conclusions.

"The Berkeley Rebels" went through an agonizing re-editing process, with Barron fighting me all the way. When it was over, I thought it was a splendid piece of work. The country badly needed some understanding of what those student demonstrations were all about. The documentary did that and more. I was proud of it and proud of the part I had played in bending it without breaking it. It also got the kind of reviews I hoped it would.

I was already giving my attention to other projects when, ten days or so after the broadcast, Fred Friendly, shaking his head, said, "Paley wants to see a tape of 'The Berkeley Rebels.'"

"What's that all about?" I asked, and quickly gathered from Fred—who had learned from Stanton—that Clerk Kerr, President of the University of California, was extremely upset by the broadcast. Well, I thought philosophically, we already knew that Kerr was angry; it had been in all the papers on the Coast. Paley and Stanton were masters at protecting the news division against attacks from outsiders, even Presidents of the United States. I would send the tape to Paley and I would never hear about it again.

No such luck. A few days later I got a call that the Chairman wanted to see me.

The meeting was very short. "I saw that 'Berkeley Rebels,'" he said. "It was the worst program I ever saw in my life."

"Well, sir," I began, as usual without stopping to think, "I'm sorry that's what you think is our worst, because that is what I think is our best." The Chairman was silent for a moment. I wondered if he might simply fire me out of hand for my intemperate reply.

"I have reason to believe part of it may have been staged."

I said I had heard the charge and was reasonably sure it was not true.

"Well, you know how I feel about that program," he said quietly.

"Yes, sir. And we'll look into it again."

The meeting was over. I reviewed the film once more and asked a lot of questions but found no way to make a satisfactory determination about the staging charges, which, of course, the people involved in the broadcast denied. I never heard another word from Paley on the subject, though Friendly may have. I always had the feeling that Bill Paley had little abiding interest in documentaries. I'm certain he believed in their efficacy, but I suspect they simply were not his cup of tea. There were so many things that he relished, that made his eyes light up, I believe I would have sensed it if he truly enjoyed our long-form programs.

A year later Arthur Barron was to produce another extraordinarily evocative and effective program, again on the theme of youth, called "16 in Webster Groves." The documentary was based on survey material gleaned from interviews with teenagers in that middle-class suburb of St. Louis. In the hands of a prosaic producer it might have been dishwater dull, but Barron made it vibrate with life, and again the charges of "staging" rang out, louder than ever. Barron and his people denied it. He was just filming what was there, he said.

In retrospect, however, one does wonder about those allegations.

Barron went on in later years to become a movie film director (probably his bent right along), entering a world in which "staging" is not the pejorative word it is in the news business. How ironic that in the theater one can win a Pulitzer Prize and in Hollywood an Emmy for staging. In the news business, a television station might lose its precious license for a flagrant staging action by its news people, and very properly so. It is the difference between the world of make-believe and the world of reality.

Nothing has been more fumbling and tortuous than the devising of practical guidelines to help documentary and hard-news producers in the field do their job in reporting on tape or film without stepping over the line into make-believe. Dick Salant, with Bob Chandler and David Klinger working under him, labored for years to specify and codify all CBS operating guidelines, occasionally some of them as honored with a wink as with an observance. The CBS News production standards on staging seem reasonably clear:

Staging is prohibited. CBS News broadcasts must be just what they purport to be. We report facts *exactly* as they occur [*sic*]. We do *not* create or change them. It is of the utmost importance, therefore, that these basic principles be adhered to scrupulously by all CBS News personnel:

—Say nothing and do nothing that may give the viewer or listener an impression of time, place, event or person which varies from the facts actually seen, heard and recorded by our equipment.

—It may be necessary, in occasional situations . . . to recreate an event for subsequent rebroadcast. In each situation, however, the fact that such a recreation is being broadcast must be made explicitly clear and . . . must be a faithful reproduction of the original event.

The problem is, as every seasoned producer, correspondent and editor knows, that it is impossible simply from a practical point of view to film or tape an extensive story without a certain amount of what could technically be construed as staging. Walking shots of a subject leaving or entering his house are a common example. It is *possible* to avoid staging completely by having the crew and director wait outside until the man appears, following the subject and repeating this procedure for several mornings and evenings until enough material is collected to serve the purpose at hand. This is all possible—but nonsensical.

In reality, a producer will generally ask the subject to leave his house, walk a few hundred feet and then go back and do it again, maybe several times. Shades of Hollywood! As written, the CBS guidelines would permit this bit of "staging" but would require mention of it in the credits. Naturally, that would make little sense.

Unfortunately, the question of staging never did—and probably never will—stop at the level of minor technical infractions. Indeed, written guidelines in this area evolved, as they did in dozens of other areas of concern, because of abuses or potential abuses over the years.

The policy of CBS News on staging, as clear and as carefully worked out as that of any news organization, contains one sentence that, had I had my wits about me, I would have tried to amend: "We report facts *exactly* as they occur." We *try* to report facts exactly as they occur. We are often nowhere near the facts, which frequently are hidden from us by those who wish to obscure them. Or, if we do know the facts, it is hellishly difficult to get them on tape—which is why producers who think they know the facts but can't aim their cameras at them go in search of a way to suggest them filmically.

Assuredly, production artistry has its place in the documentary form. I believed—and still do—that we should embrace the widest forms of subject matter, and the CBS News record shows that we did. But journalism was and should always be our main line of business. The vast majority of our documentaries, from the Murrow days on, dealt properly with timely topics. The challenge remains constant: to keep our product journalistically sound while at the same time stimulating to watch.

The late Arthur Morse, a talented *CBS Reports* producer, had the unenviable job of replacing Friendly when Fred became President of News. Arthur came a cropper over "The Ratings Game," a broadcast that caused delicate internal problems, to say the least.

In those days the debate over the efficacy, reliability and usefulness of television ratings was much hotter than it is today. When *CBS Reports* let it be known that the program would try to tackle the subject, CBS management was obviously unhappy but did not veto the decision. Early on, apparently, a vague commitment had been made by Frank Stanton that he might allow himself to be interviewed for the broadcast, but when that and other interviews with the Nielsen people failed to materialize, the project began to flounder. If it had been on a less delicate subject, the ratings project might indeed have been abandoned, but the idea that *CBS Reports* could start such a project and then give it up would certainly have invited suggestions that industry pressure—from inside or outside the company, or both—had squelched it. So the program *had* to be done.

Joe Wershba, who could shoulder any burden then and is still handling the tough ones in his sunset working years at *60 Minutes*, took over as producer. He scratched around and found enough people in the advertising and television industries to give their side of the ratings story. They included people like Rod Serling and Steve Allen, who shook their heads and allowed that slavishness to ratings was ruining the business.

It was not that we did the program so well as that we did it at all, especially inside a company where ratings were a life-and-death matter. Arthur Morse infuriated Friendly by going over his head to try to coax Stanton to appear on the broadcast (Arthur was soon to leave CBS News), and Jack Schneider, President of the CBS Television Network (who was shortly to be named President of the CBS Broadcast Group), appeared as the CBS spokesman on the subject.

It was Schneider's first "public" appearance, and he was articulate and impressive, a man marked for an important CBS future. Bob Trout narrated "The Ratings Game," which, in fact, ended up about as controversial as a bar of soap, though all the preliminary

This Is New York was a regular stop for any touring movie star in New York City with a new picture to talk about. If memory serves, Jimmy Stewart held the program record for number of appearances—seven—just edging out Danny Kaye.

I was enormously flattered to hear from James Thurber that he was a fan of my radio program in the early 1950s. We became close friends. Late in his life, nearly blind, he made few personal appearances, but he did visit *This Is New York*.

It's fair to say that Joe Louis and I were both past our prime when we sparred to a "draw" as part of the CBS promotion prior to Joe's fight with Ezzard Charles in 1952.

See It Now was the first venture into documentary television for Fred W. Friendly and Edward R. Murrow. It began in 1952, growing out of their collaboration in the *Hear It Now* radio series, which had its roots in their record album called *I Can Hear It Now.*

All the people who covered national politics in my era got to know Nelson Rockefeller—for that matter, Nelson Rockefeller got to know them.

On those few occasions when I found myself interviewing or covering Thomas E. Dewey, I kept wondering if world history might have changed appreciably if he had been elected in 1948.

After his Presidency, General Eisenhower did a number of television broadcasts for CBS. He and I became friends, and I found the real Ike to be remarkably close to the public view of him.

Eleanor Roosevelt had about her an aura of generosity, of service. She seemed constantly to be going out of her way to help others. I consider it a privilege to have known her.

To Bill Leonard — with my warm regards Eleanor Roosevelt.

2/2/58

I took Kappy and my stepson Chris Wallace along on a visit (obviously many years ago) to the late Governor Averell Harriman of New York, the first important politician Chris ever met. Nowadays, he covers the White House, and politicians crowd his life.

When I ran CBS News, Gene Jankowski, head of the CBS Broadcast Group, was my boss. He looks like someone who hasn't a care in the world. He hasn't, unless you also count the CBS Television Network, the CBS-owned stations, CBS Sports, CBS Radio . . .

This is a picture of Dick Salant and me, both laughing and happy and smiling. Radio and television news may not always be serious business, but I had to sort through a number of scowling prints before I found this one.

Trujillo was the closest the Western world had to an absolute dictator, a Caribbean Hitler. Interviewing him for an hour-long prime-time documentary, "Trujillo: Portrait of a Dictator," marked a turning point in my career.

All was peaches and cream when Don Hewitt, Walter Cronkite and I posed in front of the Cow Palace Convention Hall just before the 1964 Republican National Convention. But there were serious problems on the horizon.

Frank Stanton had an eye for the big picture, but also for the little picture. I would always take him through our convention hall set-up, and nearly always he would notice something we had overlooked.

If Harry Reasoner, sitting to the left of Lou Harris, looked a little shocked at the Oregon primary in 1964, it may be because NBC News had called the result of the election before we did.

As I announced that Dan Rather would succeed Walter as anchorman of the *CBS Evening News*, Walter himself was present to give his blessing to the new order. Within minutes, I was on my way to break the news to Roger Mudd.

Happy times at the White House, March 3, 1981. A few moments after a Cronkite interview with President Reagan, Walter is entertaining an appreciative audience (*left to right*): the author, the President, James Brady, Ed Meese, Vice President George Bush, James Baker, Bud Benjamin. (*Jack Kightlinger/The White House*)

feeling on 52nd Street was that Black Rock would probably topple when the documentary aired. Stanton himself viewed it in advance, alone—a very rare thing. The broadcast went on the air on July 12, 1965, and at the end of it Black Rock was still there.

In the 1960s and beyond, CBS News was aswarm with talented people, and by no means all of them were on the air. Friendly left *CBS Reports* with a clutch of well-trained producers. Palmer Williams as executive producer was the ringmaster who kept the documentaries flowing; Les Midgley, aided by Bernard Birnbaum, turned out news specials tied to the moment. In 1965 CBS News aired no fewer than eleven special broadcasts on the Vietnam war in prime time or late evening time.

Under my wing, but needing no guidance, was Bud Benjamin, who was winding up production of *The 20th Century*, an exceedingly successful late Sunday afternoon series. For reasons that escape me, Friendly overlooked Benjamin in his evaluation of CBS News talent, even as he more or less passed over the enormously talented Don Hewitt. While Fred was producing the hard-hitting, controversial *CBS Reports*, Bud was turning out his prize-winning weekly series, which ruffled no feathers. But whatever Bud may have lacked in crusading zeal, he more than made up for in extraordinary professionalism, fairness and decency.

From 1965, when we did our first programs together, until the end of our careers at CBS, Bud Benjamin worked with me in a variety of roles. It did not seem to make much difference what the job was—writing, producing, managing; Bud did them all with equal grace and facility. He was one of that central core of ex-newspaper people—a group that includes Midgley, Leiser, Wershba, Rooney, Cronkite and many others—who made CBS News *work*.

As it turned out, 1965 was Fred Friendly's only full year as President of CBS News. It was a year crammed with programming, some of it born of the events of the day and age (particularly the Vietnam war), some from documentaries. But perhaps the most unusual source was Friendly himself: Fred had a marvelous ability to merchandise his own ignorance. Far from being ashamed of it, he was inclined to shout it from the rooftops before millions. That was how "The National Driver's Test" originated.

Fred had received a summons that required him to spend a day learning the rules of the road, of which he was profoundly innocent. He decided on the spot to give the whole damn country a driving test. "The National Driver's Test," a sort of public-affairs quiz program, aired on May 24, 1965. It was elaborately produced, with panels in different sections of the country tested on questions of safety and driving knowledge, and the comparative results tabulated live. Shell Oil sponsored the broadcast; through its outlets, more than fifteen million test forms had reached viewers before the broadcast. People were invited to take the test on the air. There would be no prizes. The "reward," if any, was simply to find out if they could handle that basic American function, driving.

"The National Driver's Test" was produced with all the stops let out. For a CBS News broadcast, it was almost gaudy. It was heavily promoted on the air by the network itself and with newspaper advertising. And it generated a remarkable amount of press comment in advance. I remember expecting it to do well in the ratings, at least by documentary standards. But nothing like what happened. The program led every single network show, not only for that night but for a two-week period.

Perhaps the most successful producer in Friendly's original *CBS Reports* stable was the late David Lowe. His first documentary was "Harvest of Shame," which must be near the top of anyone's list of classics of the genre. In that enormously productive year of 1965, David turned out two broadcasts, "Abortion and the Law" and "The Ku Klux Klan: The Invisible Empire." The very titles suggest some of the reasons for David's high reputation. He did not write with particular grace and, unlike Arthur Barron, had no unusual talent as a field "director." Indeed, one might even question his journalistic credentials. But David Lowe was a warrior. He filmed in harm's way.

His subject matter fairly shrieked of controversy, and he was enough of a showman to sense that if a documentary was to be remembered it must penetrate to the core of the issue. Abortion: In 1965 *no one* did programs about abortion; it was a taboo subject. But Lowe, with Friendly's blessing, handled it. The Klan: Everybody talked about the Klan and its unholy influence, but David managed to get inside it, with cameras rolling. It was a sad day for the documentary form when this suave and brave practitioner of the art died suddenly in September 1965.

In 1965, too, Marvin Kalb, the former CBS News Moscow correspondent, spent months trying to get the permission of the Russian government to have us film a documentary on the Soviet Union. At that time the authorities were even edgier toward American filmmakers than they are today. But the idea that we might show Soviet life by following the course of the river Volga appealed to the Russians, and Kalb finally got the go-ahead. Gene DePoris, a feisty *CBS Reports* producer, joined him, and down the river they went.

"The Volga" was memorable on two counts: Though the authorities were looking over Kalb's shoulders as it was filmed, it was untouched by Soviet script censorship; in addition, it was the first CBS documentary ever aired in color. To American television audiences it was interesting enough, but it came across as just a bit soft on Communism. Those Russians, well, they seemed to be sort of, er, ah, ordinary people when you got to know them on their home turf, going about their business. But "The Volga" hit official Moscow like a cruise missile.

Some of Kalb's references to the way Soviet society worked— revering Lenin as a Russian God, for instance—infuriated them. There wasn't much in the film that angered them, but what was there was just enough to get the Soviet officials who had given us permission to make the film into all kinds of trouble.

Many months later, when I went to Moscow on other matters, I was given a tongue-lashing that went on for hours in almost Kafka-like sessions. Kalb was vilified. Some years later, Bill Paley himself was in the Soviet Union and was absolutely astounded when *he* was given a royal dressing-down about the broadcast. "I wasn't used to having people talk to me that way," he reported later. "It was quite surprising."

"The Volga" is an odd example, but it does seem that documentaries that do the job get some people mad. Very often the subject itself causes a stir, as with David Lowe's broadcast. And sly producers know that broadcasts tend to get attention as much for the anger they arouse as for the praise they generate, often more so. A few unscrupulous ones will deliberately distort and slant their material simply to get attention; producers of that ilk did not work for CBS News very long. Over the years Bud Benjamin, Bob Chandler and I spent much of our time trying to make sure that our producers did not stoop to controversy for its own sake.

To many men and women who toiled on them in the field, CBS News documentaries went through what certainly seemed an annoying and redundant review process. After months of research, the meat of hundreds of hours of film is boiled down to perhaps eighty minutes of material. With pride and fear struggling for first place in his heart, the producer shows it all to his immediate boss—an executive producer, a more experienced man, who may have four or five producers working under him. Inevitably, Executive Producer sees things that Producer may have overlooked: redundancies here, confusion there. Producer fights a gallant rear-guard action, but gradually his perfect product is cut where he said it could not be cut, improved where he said it could not be improved, sharpened in places where he felt it already cut right through to the bone. Finally, it is *really* perfect. But now the process starts all over again. Another gauntlet to be run. This one the worst of all: They must show the perfect product to Leonard.

I took the job of screening and reviewing and, if necessary, reshaping our documentary product very seriously indeed. Besides, it was enormously satisfying: For a few hours at least it plunged me back into the creative side of the business. In the more than ten years that documentaries were among my major responsibilities, there was only one that escaped my screening without a single suggestion for change: Jay McMullen's "The Mexican Connection." In fact, in my early days as a news executive, my expertise in the documentary area sometimes kept me in good standing with producers.

Those poor producers. Friendly and, after him, Salant (and years later I as President) routinely screened all documentaries before air time, occasionally but not often calling for still another change here or there. (Top CBS management did not, as a matter of general practice, see documentaries before they went on the air, although anyone who had the ultimate responsibility—Paley, Stanton or the head of the Broadcast Group—had the right to view the product.) Salant got deeply involved in the creative process with only one broadcast, "The Selling of the Pentagon," but not even his considerable advance care could keep it safe from attack. More on that later.

Many sales people and executives at the CBS Television Network have been interested in seeing our material in advance, but they did not until a day or two before broadcast when, like all programs, it was put on closed circuit and fed down the line to stations of the network. Every once in a while, the controversial nature of certain subject matter led affiliates not to carry a CBS documentary report; even more often they preempted for something a little "sexier," not so much because of the documentaries' content but because they lacked drawing power.

All such arcane problems—dealing with affiliates, network executives, ad sponsors—were far off in another world for the men and women who fashioned our documentaries. They had read the names and titles of the bigwigs. They knew there was a CBS Television Network; affiliates were out there somewhere; advertisers were out there somewhere, too. It was for Friendly and Salant and me to protect documentary producers against all that stuff. They were our creative army, the men who shaped what went out on the tube, at least our small part of it.

Producers. I loved most of them, but they were not perfect.

The most common error producers made was lack of clarity. I

tried to think of myself as an ordinary viewer, although of course I knew I came to most documentaries with more knowledge of the subject than most viewers. The problem, as I saw it, was that if everything wasn't crystal clear to me as I watched, then I felt certain the typical TV viewer would be confused. And I knew that if my attention was wandering, if I found myself shifting around in my seat, the fault wasn't mine; something was wrong on the screen. The documentaries usually dealt with serious material, but if they were not handled in a reasonably engaging manner no one would be watching for long, not even viewers who were willing to meet us halfway. "My ass itched," I sometimes complained, during a break in a screening. The producers and editors learned to respect that comment.

Another frequent complaint I had was that a few producers, certain that they knew most if not all the routes toward the creation of a better world, tended to load their documentary dice in the direction of those they perceived as the good guys, chasing after good causes—gun control, for instance. But Salant and I, and Benjamin and Chandler too, spent many a long hour trying to make sure that every devil got his due at air time. I'm sure some producers thought we were damned obstructionists, just out to flex our executive muscles.

The rigorous system of review at CBS News had its weaknesses. Not surprisingly, the "reviewers" did not always agree on what was wrong with a producer's effort, what needed fixing or how to fix it. And there was always the danger that the review process would rip the guts out of a documentary instead of insuring its clarity and accuracy—but those were chances worth taking. I have no doubt whatsoever that the vast majority of documentaries actually showed improvement, by almost any standard of measurement, as a result of our review process. Even so, all the pre-broadcast care possible by people who were not actually in the field or in the editing room will not insure against an outbreak of accusations against a broadcast that rubs the raw nerves of an important special interest. I daresay there has never been a documentary which, if examined under a microscope, word by word, edit by edit, could not be faulted. Once I was raked over by a Congressional subcommittee for a documentary that never even went on the air. More on that, too, later.

I never had a serious disagreement with Friendly, or later Salant, about documentaries but, left to their own devices, they might have been happier if all our documentary subject matter had been issue-oriented. I felt it was important to tackle a wide range of subjects. It was my attitude toward subject selection that largely prevailed.

To my mind, aside from film or tape of virtually immortal news events, such as the first moon walk, the program with the best chance of immortality was the one CBS News produced in 1964, a documentary entitled "D-Day Plus 20 Years: Eisenhower Returns to Normandy." It has already been repeated several times, and I am certain that on the fiftieth anniversary of D-Day in 1994 it will be played again. I was lucky enough to be on the scene for part of the making of that documentary in 1963.

That summer, as activity in my election unit slowed to a crawl between political campaigns, I was temporarily made CBS News "bureau chief" in Paris. The fact that Ike was going back to Normandy was important news, and I took a film crew along to do several stories about the documentary adventure itself. Fred Friendly was the producer (one of the rare times Fred ventured into the field); Bill Paley arrived with his friend Walter Thayer; John Eisenhower flew in from Belgium, where he was stationed. Mamie Eisenhower was there, too, and Betsy Cronkite, along with Walter, who was the documentary's correspondent.

They were all staying in a hotel in Caen, which I'd been told was a Gestapo headquarters during the war. The whole area was redolent with war history. One night, the Chairman asked us all to dinner in a private dining room of the hotel. It was my first meeting with former President Eisenhower, whom I later came to know quite well. Surrounded by good food, friends and memories, Ike was in great form that night. He and Mamie began to tell Patton stories, Ike telling how "Georgie" got down on his knees and begged the General not to fire him after he slapped that soldier. Ike imitated Patton in a squeaky little voice, and everyone thought it was funny as hell. "That Ike is something when he gets it going," I remember Mamie saying.

It was an unforgettable evening. At one point I glanced at Fred and knew he was thinking the same thing I was: Wouldn't it have been wonderful if we'd had a camera and microphone getting all this down for posterity? The actual broadcast was stunningly effective, the more so as the years have rolled on, and its hero, General of the Armies Dwight D. Eisenhower, passed into history.

After President Eisenhower left office in 1960, he participated in a number of broadcasts with CBS News, which had the edge on the other networks because of his friendship with Bill Paley. The Chairman put Friendly in touch with Ike, and for as long as Fred was at CBS he was more or less keeper of the Eisenhower keys when it came to appearances of any length. Occasionally, Fred would borrow the company plane and fly down to see the old man in Gettysburg, which was inconvenient to reach by other means, and once or twice I went with him. I would talk a little bridge and golf with the General, and that stood me in good stead when, after Fred left CBS, I inherited the role of preserving the company's link with Ike.

Toward the very end of his life, we retraced his youth in "Young Mr. Eisenhower," a remarkably touching broadcast with Harry Reasoner as commentator. We filmed half of it in Abilene, Kansas, where Ike was brought up, and the latter part at West Point. I stayed closely involved with it from beginning to end. My wife, Kappy, went with us to West Point to watch the filming and kept the General company during periods when he was not on camera. One quaintly old-fashioned moment sticks in her mind as she recalls the experience.

"What's that you're reading?" he asked, glancing at a book lying in her lap.

"The Hemingway biography, Mr. President," said Kappy.

"I see," said Ike thoughtfully. "I don't care for Hemingway. He's too *dirty*."

*   *   *

I have never understood why my bosses—almost all of whom I liked, all men who had been genuinely supportive of me—kept getting shot out from over me. Dick Swift, Sig Mickelson, Dick Salant, Jack Schneider, Arthur Taylor, John Backe, Fred Friendly.

The story of Fred's dramatic, inevitably dramatic, resignation has been recounted by numbers of journalists and by two of the principals, Fred himself and William S. Paley. Not surprisingly, their accounts do not mesh entirely. Friendly stated publicly that in the main he was motivated to resign by CBS's airing a rerun of *I Love Lucy* instead of carrying George Kennan's testimony before the Senate Foreign Relations Committee concerning Vietnam; Paley insists that the principal bone of contention between them was Fred's refusal to report to Jack Schneider rather than directly to Stanton and himself.

Gordon Manning and I were in and out of Friendly's office during the several days of high tension that finally resulted in Fred's resignation on February 15, 1966. He was indeed bitterly upset that Jack Schneider had made the decision not to carry the third day of the Vietnam hearings. Fred kept telling us he thought he would have to resign. I don't think either of us really took him too seriously until the very end, although we both sided with him on the principle of the matter: for us to carry the hearings and for CBS News to report on them as it always had.

Fred had a history of making theatrical gestures; *talking* resignation was nothing new. He was always quick to stand up to the company when he didn't think it was behaving itself. On at least one occasion he and Ed Murrow actually paid for a large *New York Times* ad for one of their broadcasts when CBS declined to do so. And now here he was threatening to quit as President of CBS News, not a job to toss aside lightly.

But toss it aside he did. He called me into his office and showed me his letter of resignation, saying the deed was done. I offered to submit mine if he thought it would help make a point, but he smiled rather sadly and said no, he thought I ought to stick around.

It may be true that by temperament Friendly was not destined to stay at CBS News much longer anyway. If it had not been that blowup, then surely, one could imagine, it would have been another. Indeed it took all the reasoned calm of Dick Salant to guide CBS News through the troubled waters of Watergate, of "Hunger in America," of "The Selling of the Pentagon." Even so, if Fred's future did not lie in CBS News, I was—and still am—sorry that an editor and producer of such extraordinary talent wasn't working somewhere at the core of the business, in the thick of the action during the sixties and seventies.

After Fred Friendly left CBS News, Gordon Manning and I stayed. And in February 1966 my old boss, Dick Salant, was welcomed back.

8

THE BIRTH OF *60 MINUTES* AND OTHER ADVENTURES

A hole had been cut in the south wall of the CBS News President's office and a door installed at the order of Fred Friendly, who thought an extra door might provide a convenient way for him to evade unwelcome visitors. When Dick Salant replaced Friendly, he quickly ordered the second door—"Friendly's door," we used to call it—boarded over. The mark of Fred W. Friendly on CBS News would remain forever, but Dick Salant wanted no reminders of him around the President's office.

Dick put back his favorite little sign, out of Shakespeare: "The first thing we do, let's kill all the lawyers." He was in business again, happy as a hog in mud. The troops of the News Division were generally relieved that, after the page-one trauma of the Friendly resignation, a known and respected presence would be in the front office. Salant had limited admiration for his predecessor and never bothered to conceal it. Friendly was far less blunt in his public and private appraisals of Salant. Their only common bond was that serious journalism as practiced by CBS News at its best ranked with God and Country in their scheme of things.

I sometimes wonder how I could have served and felt deep affection for two such disparate types, both so utterly different in temperament not only from each other but also from me. Like most brilliant men, they were erratic, and alternately difficult and splendid to work for. Curiously, I heard almost the same wisecrack made about them by two separate CBS News people. Said a *CBS Reports* producer of Friendly, "For a smart son of a bitch, he sure is dumb." And from a CBS News executive, "Salant is smart, smart, smart—except when he's dumb, dumb, dumb." To my mind, neither was dumb very often.

Salant immediately asked Manning and me to stay on in our jobs. It was astonishing. One day Fred, the next day Dick. Life went on.

Under Dick we were given considerable latitude in running our respective parts of the News division. Managing the hard-news side of things continued to be the most taxing and the most important of the two jobs, with two-thirds of what was even then, in 1966, a budget of about $100 million annually. The performance of every CBS News daily broadcast, on both radio and television, and of every bureau, every correspondent and many producers—all of it was directly or indirectly Gordon's responsibility. By the time Salant had replaced Friendly, Manning, despite a lifetime as a journalist, had barely two years of television experience. He learned quickly, though, charged with an ever-present energy and enthusiasm and good humor. We occupied a suite of offices that shared a common waiting room, and our doors were open to each other more often than not.

In most ways Salant was considerably easier to work for than Friendly. He kept regular hours and was not afraid to delegate. He had—indeed has—a fine and educated mind. And he loved the news business, for which he had no training whatsoever. Manning and I, in one of our not uncommon fits of exaggeration, once contrasted the styles of Salant and Friendly as Management by

Memo versus Management by Messiah. Salant too was a handful, but different from Friendly. Fred would often agonize over a decision dramatically. His huge hands seemed born to be wrung. Not Salant. He was decisive almost to a fault. We would get a yes or a no from Dick almost before we had finished asking the question. Occasionally Gordon and I knew he had made his decision a little too fast, and all day—sometimes singly, sometimes together—we would go into his office to try to change his mind. By late afternoon, if indeed we had been right all along, we would have him convinced. Gordon and I, both Navy men, called it "the old 180"—a 180-degree turn. The remarkable thing was that Salant was always cheerful about changing his mind. If he'd made a mistake, he would embrace his error with small-boy enthusiasm. "I goofed," he would say, beaming.

He could be orally articulate when aroused, but he was happiest writing his memos. Woe to the man or woman, inside or outside the company, who tried to tangle with him on paper. Salant, who had an organized mind and had been trained well as a lawyer, was a splendid citer of chapter and verse, and he would lay it all out, single spaced, page after page. Manning and I, with our butterfly brains, might be off and running on another crisis. Sometimes we would meet outside our offices, each clutching a copy of a three-page Salant memo, and simply look at each other, eyes rolling, particularly if Salant was demanding an immediate and detailed answer to a complicated question. To newsmen, trained to regard brevity as a virtue, Salant could seem unnecessarily prolix. But that was Dick. Much more important were his honesty and his courage.

When Friendly left CBS, my job remained nominally the same—Vice President of News Programming—but in fact it underwent a sea change. My primary responsibility, documentary programming, had been in the field from which Fred Friendly had sprung. There would be no master looking over my shoulder now. For that matter, of the top three officers now at CBS News, I had far and away the broadest television news experience, thanks to my years as a correspondent and the time I put in running the election unit. I became a kind of senior consultant on the hard-news side of our business.

In the late sixties, as the brief Friendly period yielded to the Salant era, there were documentaries still to come, controversies that would rage but were as yet unborn and, as we began anew under our new leader, we felt only the first faint stirrings of the enormous success CBS News would enjoy in the near future. A future ushered in by 60 *Minutes*.

60 *Minutes* is the most successful television series of all time, measured by almost any standard, not the least being cash flow. One year, in fact, the profit generated by 60 *Minutes* was said to have been *all* the money made in prime time by the CBS Television Network. It has been honored with dozens of awards for outstanding television journalism. It has been variously imitated—seldom with much success—by the other major network news divisions and countless local stations.

Not surprising, then, that to a few of us who labored in the less glamorous documentary side of television for many years, the avid public appetite for 60 *Minutes* gives an ironic satisfaction. The dismal cafeteria in the bowels of 524 West 57th Street was sometimes the scene of coffee-break or lunchtime speculation on whether good ratings could *ever* go hand in hand with quality non-entertainment broadcasts, or a series. The consensus was that when ratings came in the door, real journalism probably had flown out the window.

To Dick Salant, the term "show business" was like syphilis: He didn't want to catch it. Even a story that smacked of "human interest" was hardly worth our precious air time. Fred Friendly was deadly serious about what he and Murrow (and later he and his producers without Murrow) were doing, but he had somewhat less fear than Dick that attracting many viewers might dilute the purity of his product. For a long time it hardly mattered. Whenever the ratings for *CBS Reports* would come in, we would note that about half as many people watched documentaries as entertainment programs. That was life. That was the way folks out there *were*. Most of them—not all of them but most of them—would rather be entertained than informed. To get ratings, make the jokes funnier. Undress the girls. We were not in the business of making jokes at all, much less funnier.

Still, we couldn't help wondering if it might not be possible to eat our cake and have a little bit of it, too.

In the mid-sixties, CBS News was assigned—grudgingly—one prime-time hour a week to do with what it would. Well, not *quite* an hour a week. We were given a slot by the network from 10:00 to 11:00 P.M. every Tuesday for three weeks in a row; on the fourth week of the month, we were given half an hour at 10:00 P.M., with the second half of the hour turned over to the local stations, for them to perform good works in their particular area, which presumably most of them did.

The odd half hour was a bastard little segment, and we tried all manner of not very successful experiments in it, while preserving the three other hours a month for our meat-and-potatoes documentaries. The half hour, tucked in once every month, never developed continuity or character. Whenever an idea came along that didn't seem quite important enough to warrant the expense or effort of a full-hour documentary, we would let some disappointed producer do a half-hour show.

As usual, at our weekly luncheon meetings, Salant, Manning, Bud Benjamin, Perry Wolff, Bob Chandler and I would thrash out the latest crop of documentary ideas. They came from a variety of sources, but most from the stable of producers working under Benjamin and Wolff. I must admit that if either Salant or I really pushed enthusiastically for an idea that had been submitted it would soon be in the works, and that if either one of us was violently opposed it was dead.

Manning was inevitably full of ideas and enthusiasm, but he was careful not to invade my turf. One day, after our weekly documentary lunch, Gordon said to me, "You know, it's amazing how many of those ideas today might have made pretty good magazine pieces, but they weren't worth a book, which is what the producers were trying to sell."

"Yes," I agreed. "We've got a daily paper here with the *CBS Evening News,* and we publish good books with the documentaries, but we don't have any *Time* or *Newsweek.*"

The exchange immediately made me think of Don Hewitt. Don had been more or less at loose ends since Friendly fired him as executive producer of the *Evening News,* and he had fallen under my wing.

Sooner or later, anyone with Don Hewitt working for him is bound to succeed—and certain to have adventures along the way. Seeking a way to make his mark again, Don had toyed with a magazine format and talked it over with Friendly. I don't think the idea had been committed to paper. If ever there were two men in this world who shunned paper they were the two. Fred, like everyone else who has crossed Hewitt's path, had affection for Don, but he felt Don's talent lacked depth and intellectual commitment. Fred was not about to go to bat for a series, probably of any nature, with Don at the helm. I suppose that magazine-format notion could be called the seed, or one of the seeds, of *60 Minutes,* although it never came close to getting off the ground.

When Friendly departed, Don talked to me again about the idea, which still did not seem like an easy sell. Don's thoughts, and mine, were not exactly focused. Then one day in late 1967 or early 1968, I heard about an extremely hard-hitting, controversial Canadian series called *This Hour Has Seven Days.* The series, produced by Doug Leiterman, dealt with public issues and personalities and did so in a manner that had rocked the Dominion. Eventually the program was taken off the air, but not until it had racked up extraordinary ratings—for a period it was the most watched program in Canada.

Leiterman then became a documentary producer working, although not for long, for CBS News. He arranged to get a print of one of the Canadian programs down for us to take a look at, and we did—Hewitt, Bob Chandler, Bud Benjamin and I. The episode we saw was riveting, and the magazine format—three or four stories, as I recall—worked.

The only trouble was that the investigative journalism seemed to us questionable, to say the least. But the idea had taken hold: Aggressive, investigative journalism, done *responsibly*, could be handled in a fairly short form. If it included pieces that focused on personalities, with human-interest stories, such a format might constitute a broadcast of comparatively wide appeal.

Over the next several months, Don Hewitt and I became increasingly interested in the concept. There was nothing new in the idea of a video magazine, it was truly as old as television. Even my old *Eye on New York* was a kind of magazine. The great *See It Now*, forerunner of *CBS Reports*, often contained more than one story. I remember thinking again that CBS News really needed a vehicle to fill the gap that Gordon Manning and I had chatted about, the gap between the short form of the daily news broadcast and the long form of the documentary. Surely there must be a way to fill that gap, and surely Don Hewitt was the man who might be able to do it. The fact that neither he nor I nor those around us knew exactly what to do or exactly what would work didn't bother me a great deal, and I doubt that it bothered Don at all.

Don was used to making things work—things that had never been done before. There was nothing in television he had not done and done famously well, both as a producer and as a director. Too quick, too facile, too bright, too bursting with ideas—perhaps these charges were true. One of his pals once said of him, "Don always seems in such a hurry you wonder if he's trying to get to the bathroom." Sometimes he *was* too busy with the moment to think much about the moment after next. Nevertheless, I felt then, as the whole broadcasting world recognizes now, that Don Hewitt was extraordinary. Even as he bounces into his sixties I think of him as a boy of irrepressible enthusiasm and unlimited energy.

After considerable struggling, Don worked out a format for *60 Minutes* that was much more complicated than what we used ultimately. We were prepared, for instance, to go "live" and do a piece from wherever something was happening on any given Tuesday night between 10:00 and 11:00. The original format provided for just about everything of which we were capable—live, taped and filmed scenes; short pieces and long; hard and soft emphasis; outside opinion and inside commentary. At that early stage of planning, if Don had proposed what eventually turned out to be the winning format ("I'd like to do just three pieces each week on film, period"), he might have been laughed out of court.

Dick Salant had grave and legitimate reservations about Don's proposed format, based not so much on the supposition that 60 Minutes might fail but that it might indeed succeed. He treasured the documentary-hour time period wrung reluctantly from the network each year. I was the guardian of that series, and we were both proud of what it had generated, including, in some cases, national controversies. Dick would say to me, "I can't understand why you would want to give up a part of our mandate. If we did 60 Minutes, it would be at the expense of a dozen or so documentaries." He was right. We held no other prime time beyond the 10:00 P.M. Tuesday slot, and we commanded no other real public-affairs funds beyond the total pool set aside to program this time period.

My reply would be that our journalism was lopsided. There simply were not that many subjects worth an hour of coverage that had not already been treated exhaustively by CBS or the other networks over the past decade. But there were literally hundreds of stories worth from ten minutes to half an hour. I would point out how many such stories had been proposed and discussed at our weekly meetings that never saw the light of day because there was no place for them within our current programming schedule.

Dick finally agreed, but for a long time he thought the price of altering our format would be too high. You might win the battle and lose the war, he kept coming back to tell me, we might kill the documentary in the process. In the long run, he turned out to be not far from wrong.

Gordon Manning, Bud Benjamin and I all felt quite strongly that the shop needed a short-form vehicle. None of us felt overly concerned, as Dick did, that "short" and "soft" were synonymous. Like

Friendly, Dick seemed to question whether Hewitt cared deeply enough about serious journalism to warrant turning over so much time to him, brilliant as he knew him to be.

One lunchtime, as these arguments swayed back and forth, I listened to Salant's point of view again and said impishly, as was my bad habit, "You know, Dick, this is the first time I've ever heard you and Friendly agree on anything."

Salant shot me a startled look. "Is that true? Did Fred turn down something like this?"

"Absolutely," I said. "And for exactly the same reasons."

"My God," said Dick. "Maybe there's something to the idea after all." He laughed. We all laughed. And somehow the going was a little easier after that.

60 Minutes did get on the air finally, after something vaguely resembling an audition tape. There had never been any question that Harry Reasoner would be either host or cohost. The program obviously suited Harry, who never looks out of place regardless of the subject. Beyond this, if Harry was not the best writer in the whole News Division stable, he was damn close to it. But Don Hewitt and I both felt the program would be better with two hosts (today it has five!) because it would be difficult for one correspondent to bank enough pieces ahead of time to give the producer any kind of choice in putting together the best program. Then, too, we wondered if Harry alone, splendid choice though he was, could successfully be all things to all kinds of subjects—hard, soft and medium. Don, Bud and I all felt that Mike Wallace would be right for the job of cohost. Salant had his doubts.

Mike had come to CBS News without solid news credentials. He was a nationally known, and controversial, figure, with a reputation as a fearless interviewer and as a highly professional broadcaster. He had been brought in to try to rescue the CBS Morning News, and if he had not quite pulled off that miracle, he was gradually showing the rest of the shop, particularly on the floor of the 1964 conventions, that he could report with the best of them and outhustle them all.

But 60 Minutes was serious business, and Salant was justifiably cautious. I composed as persuasive a memo as I could put together on behalf of Wallace, without Mike's knowledge. No sooner did my memo hit Dick's desk than he shot off his decisive opinion: Let's go with Mike. And off we went.

On September 24, 1968, *60 Minutes* went on the air. The first piece was vintage Don Hewitt: Don had secured permission to have our cameras in the room with Richard Nixon and Hubert Humphrey—at the moment each was nominated for the Presidency—with the understanding that these intimate family scenes would not be aired until our inaugural broadcast months later. The segments did not have an ounce of political importance, but they were warmly appealing and showed obvious enterprise. Segments with Art Buchwald, Malcolm Muggeridge and Ramsey Clark also appeared on that first broadcast.

The history of *60 Minutes* has been recounted many times, with writers often implying that the series was not a success at first but gradually grew into something wildly popular. It all depends on what one calls success. As far as we who were running CBS News were concerned, it was a smash almost immediately. Within two seasons it had won a Peabody and a DuPont Award, and from the very first year its ratings were somewhat higher than the documentaries that aired on our other Tuesday nights. Mike Wallace quickly established himself as the essential on-camera ingredient of the series, sometimes using interview techniques that shocked viewers, bosses and colleagues alike. Over the years Wallace and Hewitt have become the linchpins that hold *60 Minutes* in place.

Harry Reasoner left CBS News after a couple of years, and went over to ABC. I must admit I had a lot to do with his unhappiness at CBS. Harry had been one of the key people broadcasting our coverage of the 1966 midterm elections, of which I was in charge. He turned in what I, and others, thought was a second-rate job. The Harry of wit, the Harry of style, the Harry of shrewd observation were all eclipsed by the Harry of comparative ignorance. He simply had not done his homework. And I told him so.

Reasoner suggested not that he'd merely had an off night but rather that homework was not his strong suit. If that was the case, I thought, he had better not be broadcasting on election night. When the 1968 Presidential election rolled around, I saw to it, with the concurrence of Salant and Manning, that Harry was not assigned to the broadcast.

Though Harry became anchor of the ABC News evening broadcast, his heart, like those of so many others who left, remained at CBS. He continued to have his hair cut at the little barbershop in our West 57th Street basement. Superb broadcaster that he is, he did a great deal for ABC's legitimacy and popularity. (Happily, for both Harry and CBS News, he was back home and back at 60 Minutes in a few years.)

In occasional fits of self-delusion, I like to think that I made many more friends than I lost as a senior executive at CBS News. As a former correspondent, I always found it distasteful to be the "boss" of former colleagues, particularly those I admired. Harry was one of them, and I am afraid I lost him. When I run into him occasionally now, he gives me a sad, shy look that seems to say "What a pity." That's the way I feel, too.

When Harry left CBS News, it was obvious to me that the man to replace him was Charles Kuralt. (Imagine a place so rich that we had someone like Charles Kuralt waiting in the wings!) "Charlie, you've been 'on the road' for a long, long time. Now let's move forward. 60 Minutes awaits you." But the answer came back, "No." A firm, polite "No." Charlie preferred—we thought, against all reason—to shuffle along the sweet backways of America in his own fashion. That put us back to square one. We all weighed in with suggestions; none seemed to fit. One day Hewitt and I got to talking about Morley Safer, who was then stationed in London. His name was far from a household word, but everyone at CBS News remembered him for extraordinary work under fire in Vietnam some years earlier, highlighted by his coverage of the controversial Cam Ne incident in which a group of Marines torched a village while our cameras told the tale.

Safer's pieces from Europe had two outstanding qualities. First, they were exceedingly well written. Second, they *moved*. Most reporters tend to stand in one place and let the camera wander around. With Morley, one got the sense that he was really *covering* the story and that the camera had better hurry to keep up with him.

Don Hewitt and I became convinced that these were enormous assets for a *60 Minutes* reporter. So what if he was not well-known? He would be. And he was not exactly pretty. Well, you can't have everything. To the surprise of many and the misgivings of a few, Morley Safer joined Mike Wallace. Morley fulfilled his promise, and then some. It was a move no one ever regretted.

A series of canny executive decisions made by Jack Schneider, the late Bob Wood, Oscar Katz and other executives at the CBS Television Network moved *60 Minutes* over a period of several years into varying time slots, first to 6:00 P.M. on Sunday, where it showed broad appeal but suffered from blackouts during the football season, and finally to full flower at 7:00 P.M. on Sunday. The folks out there in TV land had gotten to know the series better thanks to a Schneider gamble that prime-time exposure during the summer repeat season, when entertainment competition was less, would introduce Wallace and Company to a whole new set of viewers.

Among the executives at Black Rock, opinion was by no means unanimous, however, that the program should be moved from 6:00 to 7:00 P.M. "You have the perfect show in the perfect time period. Why would you want to fool around with it?" went one strong argument. At News, our feeling was that whatever risk there might be in moving into prime time (prime time starts at 7:00 P.M. on Sundays) was far outweighed by the blessing of being on the air fifty-two weeks a year—and not drowned by football mania. Jack Schneider, then President of the Broadcast Group, and others, recognized another very important factor that spoke for the move: FCC regulations made it possible to schedule only children's or public-affairs programs in the 7:00 to 8:00 P.M. time period.

But conventional wisdom was that no news-produced, public affairs–oriented program could cut the mustard against Walt Disney or other popular family entertainment. There were CBS Research Department studies that showed it couldn't be done; the figures shook even Dick Salant. Nevertheless, Oscar Katz, a fan of 60 Minutes, had seen research "figures" that turned out to be wrong too many times in the past to be impressed. He paid more attention to what the series had done during its two summers (1970 and 1971) in prime time, and he lobbied strongly for the move to 7:00 P.M.

Schneider's decision to go ahead with 60 Minutes at 7:00 P.M. must rank as one of the most critical in television history. It would not have meant a thing, of course, if the product had not lived up to the promise it had already begun to deliver. But it did. And the impossible happened: In its first year at its new time, 60 Minutes easily won its time period. By its second year it ranked among the top ten most popular programs on the air. By its fourth year in the 7:00 P.M. time slot, it was the most watched program in America.

Some of its early supporters in the press, who had called it the greatest thing since the first English muffin, began to take a second look. Hey, we know it's news, we know it's public affairs—but it's so damn popular it's got to be *entertainment!* And if it's entertainment, it can't be news and public affairs. Or can it?

Long before serious critics began reexamining 60 Minutes for this and other perceived faults, including hot-pursuit interviews, those of us who were guardians of the series tried to make sure that the show did not stray far from the straight and narrow. We set up a system whereby subject matter was approved in advance, not only to avoid duplication with other CBS News projects but also to make sure that serious content and subject matter of genuine import made up most of the assignments.

Mike Wallace and Morley Safer turned out to be our best watchdogs in the war against fluff. They were never better—or happier—than when in hot pursuit of tough and difficult stories, some at the ends of the earth, a few on the edge of real danger. I certainly never imagined that the series would evolve, as it gradually did, into a Richard Harding Davis–Lincoln Steffens sort of television journalism, with viewers often identifying more with the reporters than with the stories they reported. No one connected with the series really had that in mind.

In the early years, Don Hewitt kept trying to complicate the broadcast, looking for more and better "little" features that would keep audiences glued to their sets. Don kept wanting to try cartoons on the air, and once in a while, against my better judgment, I let him have his way. They were a mess. My own suggestions were uniformly so bad that I have conveniently forgotten them. The only segments that ever worked as features involved viewers' mail and Andy Rooney. Both came about more or less by accident.

One of Dick Salant's qualities was—and is—a high sense of what's right, fair and just, a sense that sometimes ran afoul of fast-paced programming. He insisted that 60 Minutes should give over some time to viewer reaction, a notion that always caused Don Hewitt's eyes to glaze. "Not that again," he'd plead. "That again," I told him. Don, ever the good soldier, would grab a handful of mail, extract a phrase here and a phrase there and put together a now-you-see-it-now-you-don't mail package, never quite meaty enough to satisfy either Salant or me, but apparently just right for the viewers. The mail segment has been a weekly feature of 60 Minutes since before some of today's regular watchers were born.

Andy Rooney is one of the most ambitious men I have ever known in my life. When you combine that degree of ambition with a virtually unlimited capacity to turn out fresh material on a type-writer, ream after ream, day after day, year after year, you have a winner. The odd part of his story is that it took him so long to get to be the Andy Rooney we know. For donkey's years he was a television writer's writer, so good that even Harry Reasoner would let Andy write for him and you couldn't tell the difference. Andy was without side and without sham. And he despised it in others. He liked people who could write and who appreciated good food. In 1950 he looked about the same as he does now. Unmade.

He came into his own in 1973 with a one-hour broadcast called "Mr. Rooney Goes to Washington" that managed to be satiric, funny and mildly investigatory at the same time. Oddly enough, the idea that he should turn his attention to Washington and amble through the mess down there was not his, and he resisted the subject at first. Finally he accepted the assignment with pursed lips, went down to the capital, and turned out a small masterpiece.

The short end-pieces he began doing for *60 Minutes* late in 1978 alternated with a feature within the program called "Point-Counterpoint," in which Shana Alexander and Jack Kilpatrick, among others, as liberal and conservative opponents, would somewhat artificially go at each other for a couple of minutes. When "Point-Counterpoint" had run its course in 1979, Rooney took over. He has been a fixture ever since, and I would venture to say he is the most recognizable personality of the whole *60 Minutes* crew, with the possible exception of Mike Wallace.

Rooney was a tough man to edit. Sometimes, of course, he needed editing, even as old Will Shakespeare did, but he was none too happy about it. "Yeah, I guess you're right," he would say, but usually that meant "I'll get you the next time."

Unlike the laid-back Andy Rooney, Mike Wallace had a habit of pursuing his job to the point of physical and mental exhaustion and then complaining that he was overworked. Annually there was a scene in my office that not even occasional applications of cold cash could assuage. When it became clear that a third reporter was in order, the right and obvious choice was Dan Rather. Rather had been host of *CBS Reports* documentaries for a while since leaving the post that brought him considerable fame and controversy, White House correspondent during the Nixon presidency. Everyone knew Dan would do well in the job, but, with that streak of suspicion clouding his nature, Rather wondered whether he was somehow being shunted aside rather than promoted. Salant was happy enough moving Rather to *60 Minutes*—not as pleased as he would have been if Dan had been a woman. Dick was fiercely determined to increase the number of women in both high places and low at CBS News. "Isn't there a qualified woman?" he would say. "No," I would answer, "not since Michele Clark died," referring to the tremendously talented black correspondent killed a few years earlier in a Chicago air crash—and the people on the hard-news side of the shop, those who managed the daily blood and guts of CBS News, became reconciled to the loss of Dan.

In more recent years, of course, Dan has gone on and up from the program. Harry Reasoner has come back. A cynic might say that

Ed Bradley and Diane Sawyer have provided the "balance" the hitherto white male series needed.

I was very close to 60 Minutes from its conception and birth to its adolescence and much of its prime. If Don Hewitt was its father, I was perhaps its uncle. I look at it now with an odd mixture of pride and concern. Pride that I was a part of something that has been excellent so often for so long in front of so many. Concern when, as sometimes happens, its journalism is shoddy or it seeks merely to be attractive.

I said many years ago, when it first began to show all the signs of success, that 60 Minutes would probably stay on the air long after it deserved to be taken off. What I meant was that if the program's quality truly disintegrated, CBS News could never cancel it for that reason. Only poor ratings will do that—some far distant day, probably in the twenty-first century. That will be a financial, not a journalistic, decision, as, sadly, so damn many decisions in the television business have come to be.

Along with the high energy level characteristic of many of the dominant figures with whom I worked at CBS News over the years, there was one other quality that I particularly admired: personal courage. Morley Safer, for instance, not only survived several exceedingly dangerous stints in Vietnam but managed to film an entire documentary inside mainland China under the very noses of the authorities. Safer, a Canadian, posed as a tourist, as did his cameraman. The result was "Morley Safer's Red China Diary," a remarkable document at the time. (The film was made in 1967, before Ping-Pong diplomacy had begun to break the ice between our two countries.) Safer, of course, was only one of hundreds of television, radio and print journalists who later showed extraordinary courage in covering the Vietnam war.

Some gave their lives, and I am still haunted by my inadvertent part in the fate of one CBS News cameraman, Ramnik Lekhi. I was passing through New Delhi on my way home from the Far East when I got a call from the CBS film stringer in town, begging to meet me in the lobby of my hotel. With tears just below the surface of his huge dark eyes, Lekhi told me I was his last hope of getting a regular job with CBS News. He would go anywhere and do anything. Being a stringer was meaningless, he said, because there was so little news in New Delhi.

"Well, Lekhi," I said, "I really don't think there is much chance. But when I get back I'll tell them about you."

"Oh, I have written, sir. I have written. Many, many times. But they do not seem to understand. I am a very fine cameraman."

"I'm sure you are," I said. "By the way, would you be willing to go to Vietnam?"

"Oh, yes sir," said Lekhi. "Anywhere at all."

I made some notes, and when I got back to New York I read them to Casey Davidson, the right man to talk to about such things. A few months later I was pleased to hear that Lekhi had been hired and was working in Vietnam.

But then the sad news came. Lekhi and three other courageous CBS News people were killed in an ambush in Cambodia.

In terms of courage in the face of high danger, it may be unfair to single out one CBS News producer from the documentary ranks—particularly when, on the hard-news side, risk is a constant companion of cameramen, correspondents and producers in the field. But Jay McMullen is a special case. In World War II he had been a volunteer ambulance driver with the British Eighth Army, then a U.S. Army correspondent in Italy; later he saw action filming documentaries during the Korean War.

McMullen was a loner. He might say casually, for instance, as he did one day to his immediate CBS News boss, Bud Benjamin, "I've got some contacts with our border police trying to stop some of this drug traffic coming up from Mexico. I'd like to follow it up." A few months later, we'd have sound and film, grainy but real, with Jay in the midst of a ring of heroin-running desperadoes deep in Mexico.

Jay would never be mistaken for Robert Redford, but good looks was all he lacked to typify the very best of the new breed of reporter-producers at CBS News and the other networks. If he had a fault, it was that he was almost maddeningly meticulous, not unlike the artist who was asked how long it took him to paint a picture and who replied that he didn't know—sometimes forever.

Sometimes it seemed to take Jay McMullen forever, but the results were always worth it. Ed Murrow narrated Jay's classic early radio documentaries, "The Galindez-Murphy Case" and "Who Killed Michael Farmer?" His second television documentary, "Biography of a Bookie Joint," shook Boston to its foundations. A federal officer investigating charges growing out of the broadcast was run down and nearly killed; a cameraman narrowly escaped another hit-and-run attempt. As usual, Jay had walked in harm's way to accomplish his job, filming illicit operations often with hidden cameras.

With the possible exception of "Biography of a Bookie Joint," none of Jay McMullen's numerous feats of investigative reporting brought the kind of attention accorded him by the "Project Nassau" affair, an effort that did not result in a broadcast at all but instead cost him four grueling days behind locked doors on the witness stand before a House Investigations Subcommittee, to say nothing of several hours of rough treatment from me. "Project Nassau" is worth recalling in some small detail, not because it was CBS News's finest hour—it was not—but because it illustrates how heavy lies the hands that can be laid upon the investigative reporter and upon the organization that supports him. They may find themselves under attack, not only in advance of broadcasts, but even when there is *no* broadcast.

From the time of the clandestine Bay of Pigs fiasco in 1961, CBS News had been interested in exile activities in the Miami area, in Caribbean invasion plots and gunrunning from the U.S. In May 1966, McMullen learned of plans to smuggle guns from the U.S. to the Dominican Republic, the weapons reportedly to be used later in a planned invasion of Haiti. Cubans among the invasion group were to use Haiti as a base for assaults on Cuba. McMullen tried to show some of this activity—in the Miami area, where weapons were shown being loaded into trucks in the Cuban community; in New Jersey, where exile training included rifle practice; in Georgia, where quantities of arms and an American gun dealer were filmed.

Over a period of time, and after a host of complications, including injury to one of the exile trainees while the CBS News crew was filming, McMullen himself began to question the authenticity of some of the exile activities and to wonder if CBS News was being used. But he was never quite sure that the effort should be abandoned. I remember pressing him: The project had gone on so long, with such indifferent results, shouldn't he be moving on to something else? Finally, I decided we had better take a look at what material he had and make a decision about whether to continue or quit.

Bob Chandler, Bud Benjamin and, as I recall, Dick Salant looked at a rough cut of the "Project Nassau" material with me. The decision was easy: Scrap it. The material was thin; we didn't like the look of it. One is always taking a chance dealing with oddball characters, and "Project Nassau" was chockablock with them. It had cost CBS News perhaps $100,000 thus far—money down the drain. We thought no more about it.

But many months later, in 1971, a man then employed by CBS News who had worked on the project laid a series of well-publicized accusations before a staff member of the House Investigations Subcommittee, alleging that CBS had financed an invasion of Haiti, and a kind of witch hunt was on.

The nasty, accusatory hearings finally were put to bed with a report forwarded to the FCC, which quite properly declined to take any action whatsoever against CBS. But the recommendations of the Subcommittee report were so wildly threatening to the very principles of the American free press that they are worth quoting here if only to illustrate what loose cannons can fire in the halls of Congress:

"These facts clearly indicate the need for new legislation in the communications field which would accomplish the following objectives: (a) protect the public against falsification and deception in the preparation [sic] and presentation of purportedly bona fide news programming, and (b) prohibit the practice of news media involvement in criminal activities."

It seemed to me then, as it seems to me now, that the CBS News process had worked well in "Project Nassau," admittedly using it as a worst-case example. Investigative reporting, always a risky and delicate business, had not been discouraged; but when the material did not come up to our standards the project was abandoned.

If "Project Nassau" was not Jay McMullen's finest effort, the broadcast he was working on at the same time may indeed have been. Called "The Tenement," it aired in February 1967 and was a touching, stunning piece of work. McMullen had rented a room in a Chicago tenement house and simply filmed the life and times of the folks who lived there, a crummy place where they made do.

I know there are dozens of courses scattered around the land in documentary filmmaking and on the "art" of the documentary. Teachers of such courses could do far worse than shape one simply around the work of Jay McMullen. One could start with "The Tenement," and be sure to include "The Corporation," "Campaign American Style" and "The Selling of the F-14." They form the core of his fine legacy.

9

A WORLD
OF DOCUMENTARIES

Dick Salant wanted to create a climate conducive to the best sort of journalists, but he was generally more uncomfortable than I with talented offbeat documentary producers who might be longer on imagination than they were on objective journalism. I always liked having a few of them around, though preferably on a short leash.

It might be unfair to characterize Martin Carr as simply an off-beat type; he was occasionally erratic, yet brilliant. Martin and I went back a long time. I first knew him as program assistant and eventually as director of my *Eye on New York* broadcasts, but he had progressed from there. At CBS News, Carr was one of the first producers we would turn to for our onward-and-upward-with-the-arts documentaries, the kind of program Lou Hazam did so well at NBC. Marty produced "beautiful" broadcasts, of which "The Search for Ulysses" was a good example.

In a shop where producers of "beautiful" broadcasts were held in generally low esteem, Carr ached to prove that he could deliver the goods as a journalist. Late in 1967 he pleaded for a chance to do a film concerning poverty in our great land of plenty. I was not very impressed when he made his proposal. Documentaries about the underclass were then, as they are now, a familiar and normally "safe" serious subject. I myself had done half a dozen of them with New York City as the setting. Nevertheless, I gave Marty the go-ahead. "Hunger in America," broadcast in May 1968, was repeated less than a month later, so enormous was its impact. It became one of the most praised—and most controversial—documentaries of all time.

The broadcast was loosely based on a study by Professor Robert Coles of Harvard that described pockets of extreme poverty existing close to areas of great wealth. Cole's work attracted no popular attention. It took television to open the eyes of the country.

"Hunger in America" startled viewers accustomed to the make-believe world of American prime-time television with a shattering opening scene: a hospital nurse working over the pathetically emaciated body of a baby, as Charles Kuralt's rich, convincing voice delivered a stinging commentary: "Hunger is easy to recognize when it looks like this. This baby is dying of starvation. He was an American. Now he is dead."

That opening sequence, filmed in the nursery for premature babies at the Robert Green Hospital in San Antonio, Texas, was not only the most gripping but the most controversial scene in the broadcast. Initial viewer reaction was tremendously positive. Americans were shocked that so many could starve, or nearly starve, in their land of plenty. Thousands of unsolicited dollars poured into CBS, some from people who were far from wealthy themselves but had been so touched they simply felt they must do something.

In the case of certain documentaries, the producers and the executives above them stand braced for the controversy they are certain lies ahead when special-interest groups may be affected. Such sensitive broadcasts get enormous advance scrutiny. Years of experience had given me pretty good antennae about such things. And when the subject was particularly sensitive it was not unusual to be on the receiving end of protests of unfairness, staging or whatever, *before* air time—anything to keep the program off the air. As a matter of fact, there is no more certain way to make sure that a broadcast *does* get on the air than publicly to protest it in advance. In such cases the News department in question is fully aware that the broadcast press would be in full cry, charging that it had bowed to outside pressure if it failed to air the program in question. However, the ensuing sound and fury against "Hunger in America" took me entirely by surprise.

Most of it came from San Antonio, setting of the opening segment, which graphically showed the poverty among Mexican-Americans who make up a large percentage of the population of the city. The attacks on "Hunger in America" began with a piece in the *San Antonio Express-News* questioning whether the baby shown on the broadcast had indeed died of malnutrition. Congressman Henry B. Gonzalez, from that area, seized on "Hunger in America" as a whipping boy and managed to get a subcommittee of the House to hold hearings on the broadcast, peppering the *Congressional Record* with diatribes against CBS News. Secretary of Agriculture Orville Freeman called the broadcast "a disgraceful travesty of facts."

Positive reactions to the broadcast continued nevertheless. Senator Joseph Clark urged that the program be shown in every high school and college in the country. Indeed, within a month after the program aired, the Agriculture Department announced that its monthly surplus food package would be increased by about forty percent. When asked if the broadcast had anything to do with this, Secretary Freeman was quoted as saying, "Well, it doesn't hurt to be pushed." Meanwhile, Congressional investigation or no, a food processing plant in Duluth donated forty-five tons of food, a railroad offered free use of its boxcars for food transportation and a black boy in Alabama whom we had shown as spending a quarter for lunch got enough money through viewers' donations to eat decent lunches for well over a year.

If we had rubbed Congressman Gonzalez the wrong way, we had

surely rubbed many Americans the right way. Press comments were also favorable: One read, "When next the impatient viewer feels the urge to throw a shoe at his television set, let him remember 'Hunger in America.' CBS has reason to be proud."

The FCC conducted a preliminary staff investigation into two charges leveled against the broadcast, one involving whether the infant shown at the start of the program was indeed a victim of malnutrition, the other that we had tried to put words in the mouth of a San Antonio doctor. It found no basis for proceeding further.

As a CBS executive, I was of course proud of the impact of the broadcast. I am saddened, however, by the fact that nearly two decades later "Hunger in America" could probably be remade, perhaps even in those places where it was shot originally, and that the level of poverty in America would hardly be different.

The attacks on "Hunger in America" were like papal blessings, compared to the onslaughts that greeted what must surely rank as one of the two or three most famous documentaries of television history, "The Selling of the Pentagon." First broadcast on February 23, 1971, it was produced by Peter Davis, who had started at CBS News as a researcher and had later been Martin Carr's associate on "Hunger in America."

The origins of the documentary are curious. In mid-1970 Bud Benjamin's attention had been called to a film made by the Atomic Energy Commission on the peaceful uses of nuclear energy. "I was just bowled over by the extraordinary film footage," Bud recalled. "Incredible, I thought. Why can't we get film like that? Just as I finished screening it, Salant drifted into my office."

Salant was not an overly "visible" President, but one way he tried to keep in touch with the troops was simply to wander coatless, often with a shirttail hanging out, through the dingy hallways of the old Sheffield milk plant that housed us at CBS News, poking his nose in this or that office, chatting cheerily.

"Hey, Dick," said Benjamin, with the controlled professional enthusiasm that always registered a few decibels below Don

Hewitt's, but was no less convincing. "I just saw something absolutely *terrific*. What a piece of film! Want to see a few minutes?" Salant said sure.

Bud showed him the Atomic Energy Commission film.

"That must have cost a fortune," said Salant afterward. "Who paid for that?" Rhetorically. Knowing the answer.

"Well, the Atomic Energy Commission," Benjamin said with some hesitation. "In the long run, the taxpayer."

"We ought to do something about that," Salant replied.

Bud talked to me, and I saw immediately that there might be— probably was—a story worth documenting on film: the government's efforts to sell itself to its own taxpayers, using the taxpayers' money to do so. A research report confirmed what we were broadly aware of: Many millions were being spent by various departments of the government selling itself to the public. We asked Peter Davis to look into this explosive subject, and after some weeks he reported that all the other "selling" efforts of all other government agencies put together paled in comparison to what was being spent by the Defense Department alone in its all-out public relations effort.

Early in his research Davis had come across a book on the subject written by the former head of the Senate Foreign Relations Committee, J. William Fulbright. Very broadly, the Fulbright book became the basis for "The Selling of the Pentagon." Later, Senator Fulbright was said to have complained with rueful good grace that here was a perfect example of the power of television versus the written word. No one had paid much attention to his little book, on target though it may have been, but as for "The Selling of the Pentagon"—wow!

Davis, an engaging young man and a gifted filmmaker, put together a documentary that was stunningly effective, or wickedly one-sided, depending on one's point of view. What had started as a broadly conceived idea to look into the general extent of government public relations had become focused into a precise and quite graphic delineation of how the Vietnam war was being sold to Americans, at our own expense. This was at a time, early in 1970, when the Vietnam war was at its most controversial, the nation bitterly divided.

Unlike "Hunger in America," the volume of reaction to which took us somewhat by surprise, "The Selling of the Pentagon" seemed from the very start a broadcast that would raise almighty hell. In all my years supervising such matters, I never knew of a documentary so carefully examined in advance by CBS News management. Dick Salant, who normally stayed clear of the creative process (although always screening documentaries a week or two before they went on the air, after I had said I was satisfied that the producing team had done all it could), involved himself quite early in the screening process, sensing that efforts would be made to pounce on any small errors, to publicize and magnify them in an effort to destroy the thrust of the broadcast as a whole. This, of course, is exactly what happened.

We were so wary in advance that I remember asking Peter Davis, who had been a researcher before he graduated into the producer ranks, "Have you carefully checked every single fact and figure in this broadcast?" He said he had. "Well," I told him, "go back, and start from scratch and do it all over again." He groaned and promised it would be done.

The planned air date of the program was postponed for weeks by the extra checking, screening and reviewing process—and by one small but touchy internal problem. We discovered that in the past well-known broadcasters had commonly been hired to narrate government films, and one such film had employed our own Walter Cronkite. It seemed to some, Walter included, that we were going out of our way to inflict damage on ourselves in public if we included a clip from that film in "The Selling of the Pentagon." A clip was included. I never heard any comment on it at all, but you can be sure it would have been a part of the ammunition hurled at CBS if we had suppressed it.

"CBS Reports: The Selling of the Pentagon" had hardly left the air when it was greeted on the one hand by critical raves from the television press (it later swept the top awards for 1971) and on the other hand by concerted attacks from Washington, led by two officials, who, according to later reports, had not even seen it: Representative F. Edward Hebert, Chairman of the House Armed Services Committee, who called it "a professional hatchet job," and Vice President Spiro T. Agnew, who referred to "alleged facts which are untrue."

"The Selling of the Pentagon" was most telling when it was not dealing with facts, but simply letting its camera pan—over a bunch of youngsters roaming happily at large among military hardware, for example. And that, I suppose, is what so angered the Defense establishment: In the very midst of losing the Vietnam war, when it needed to look good and needed broad-based support, the Defense establishment came across as the bad guy.

CBS was accused of deception, particularly in the editing of an interview with Assistant Secretary of Defense Daniel Z. Henkin. The outpouring of criticism was so extensive that a couple of weeks after presenting the broadcast we repeated it, including an accusatory statement by Representative Hebert as well as a defense by Dick Salant.

But that was far from the end of the matter. Our old friends on the Investigations Subcommittee of Representative Harley O. Staggers's Commerce Committee—the same men who had tried so hard to bury us with "Project Nassau"—were back in action again, this time with a subpoena demanding all outtakes and other materials not used in the broadcast.

Television film and tape outtakes are, in a very real sense, the equivalents of a newspaper reporter's notes. On this basis—that there should be no line drawn between freedom of the broadcast press and the print press under the First Amendment of the Constitution—CBS and Frank Stanton drew the line and refused to turn over unused material from "The Selling of the Pentagon." As Stanton said at the time, "No newspaper, magazine or other part of the press could be required constitutionally to comply with such a subpoena with respect to material gathered by reporters in the course of a journalistic investigation but not published."

Frank Stanton stood his ground, and Harley Staggers stood his. An extraordinary drama now played itself out. The Committee recommended that Stanton, perhaps the most distinguished man in all broadcasting, be cited for contempt of Congress, a charge that carried, upon conviction, a possible jail sentence.

The debate in the House was heated, and there was intense lobbying behind the scenes on both sides. For the recommendation of a Congressional committee not to be supported by the full body was virtually unheard of, a shocking slap at its Chairman. On the other hand, all this was clearly a crucial showdown vote on Congress's right to poke its nose into news content in broadcasting.

At first the betting was that CBS would lose. One CBS News man who fancied himself a shrewd political observer said he was sure of it. The Democratic majority, many of them conservative, would split down the middle, he argued, while the Republicans would surely vote against CBS. He was wrong. The final vote was 226 to 181 in favor of returning the citation to the Commerce Committee. I did not know at the time, but was later told, that the Nixon White House finally passed the word that Stanton should not be cited. The feeling was that to do so would be too disruptive to the country. And was the outcome also partly the result of shrewd horse sense on the part of the man residing at 1600 Pennsylvania Avenue? Was not the year before a national election a bad time to get broadcasters angry?

At any rate, CBS won.

Any short list of men and women who over the years have made CBS News documentaries memorable would surely include Perry "Skee" Wolff, who has personally been responsible for more than a hundred special broadcasts—a number of them so good that a Perry Wolff retrospective was held at the Museum of Modern Art not long ago.

Striking a proper balance between cultural and issue-oriented matters was always difficult for me. We had one hour a week of prime time. A case could be made that with the agonies abroad in the nation and the world it was preposterous to waste it on hearts-

and-flowers material. But Wolff, with his extremely deft filming and phrasing, helped give our schedule variety and balance. He produced "Our Friends the French" and later collaborated with Luigi Barzini on "The Italians." "A Tour of the White House" with Jacqueline Kennedy, one of the captivating broadcasts of its time, made his early reputation.

Wolff had a number of producers working under him at one time or another, and was at his best taking material someone else had shot in the field and massaging it in the editing room, or finding extraordinary moments from thousands of feet of old film and then providing a narration track that was a penetrating history lesson, as in *1945* and *1968*.

Skee has produced so many memorable broadcasts in a cultural vein, his writing is so elegant, his tastes so cosmopolitan that it probably would surprise most people at CBS News to learn that his first job with the network was as producer of the *CBS Morning News*. Thus, if he so wishes, he can head a very long list of determined producers and correspondents who have tried to put CBS News on top in the morning, and failed.

I find myself coming back to that incredible year—1968. At CBS News we were acutely aware of what the nation was going through, of course: the murders of Bobby Kennedy and Martin Luther King, Jr., the black riots, the exploding passions against the war in Vietnam.

There was genuine concern in the so-called "leadership" community, black and white, that the nation might not get through the summer of '68 without devastating explosions in black areas as the hot weather arrived, perhaps much more serious even than the riots following the King assassination. Salant, Manning and I talked about this at length. Salant felt particularly strongly that here was one rare instance when we should use the time we were given in our powerful medium to try to help ease the situation. Accordingly, we decided to produce a three-part series called *Of Black America* in prime time in July of that summer.

Perry Wolff produced the first of these broadcasts, which was far and away the most memorable one. Titled "Black History: Lost, Stolen or Strayed," it starred Bill Cosby—way back when—in an absolutely marvelous scene with a group of small black children in a classroom that was intimate and touching. White critics hailed the broadcast, but, more important, so did black leaders.

Andy Rooney once wrote, "In the news division tears take precedence over laughter and there is a widespread and firmly held belief that humor lessens the importance of anything it touches. As a result of these and other things, I am one of the least important producers in television." That was in 1967—before he became "Andy Rooney." Of course he was right, or at least three-quarters right. Pompous as I am sure we were, it did seem as if the time we were allotted was simply too precious to be thrown away on trivia. Unless it was in the hands of resident genius. Such as Rooney.

But for a *serious* place, under a *serious* man, doing *serious* work, the atmosphere around the top side of CBS News was often nicely irreverent. Bud Benjamin, the senior executive producer, keeping a perfectly straight face, once mentioned to me a proposal that we do a documentary on homosexuality among white rats. "I like the idea," I said, without missing a beat, "except the black rats would be all over us asking for equal time." "The good ideas always get nibbled to death around here," Bud concluded, shaking his head sadly.

The job was *fun*. Friends, sometimes reporters, kept asking me if I missed being on the air. I did not. The job I had was incalculably more varied and interesting. In return for somewhat less attention from headwaiters and no requests for autographs, I was involved with *everything* at CBS News, or very nearly everything, instead of the much smaller turf over which a correspondent roams. Then, too, as a broadcaster in his late fifties or sixties, I might be washed up. As an executive, however, I was still learning my craft and enjoying it as the 1970s rolled in along with my middle age. My continuing responsibility for conventions and elections was another bonus: It kept me from isolation in the documentary side of the shop. (The convention and election preparation never really stopped, but I was no longer the hands-on manager.) The process of fighting for every dollar we thought was necessary to do the job—that process I was inevitably and deeply engrossed in. There the fun ended; I hated it. But it went with the territory.

There are a few variations in the budget process, company to company, year to year, but not many. Basically, the boys and girls down the line try to get as much as they can, and what they ask for gets chopped at and whittled as it moves up the line. Then, when the whole agonizing process, one royal pain in the ass, is complete, orders come from on high, to cut an additional arbitrary five, ten, fifteen or twenty percent. What's left is usually enough. Or, if it is not, the blame never falls on top management—who slashed past the fat and into the bone—but always on the smaller, working organization that was supposed to go out and get the job done. 'Twas ever thus.

In spite of the agonies of budget construction and the long dismal hours of budget cutting, I was lucky to have been at CBS when, in general, times were good and the hope was that if we could present a good enough case we could get whatever money we needed to do the job right.

In retrospect, some would say that in the documentary side of CBS News we lived in a fool's paradise in those days, with a prime-time period set aside each week for news specials of one sort or another. "The competitive environment simply won't stand that in this day and age" goes the refrain. Maybe so. But it worked then. Ironically, we were given those time periods as the result of a public promise by Frank Stanton following the quiz scandals, but gradually the commitment has eroded. I very much doubt that we will ever get it back.

Which brings me to a documentary that I confess was my idea, and that any number of my friends at Black Rock put into the category of biting the hand that feeds you. "Leonard," one of them said to me, "I thought you controlled the subject matter of those goddamn documentaries over there. What, are you crazy?" The program was called "You and the Commercial." It struck me as a simple and fit subject for us to look at, and it still does. Every human being in the United States is exposed to and affected by television commercials. Commercials are *interesting*, whether morally good, bad or indifferent. How are they made? Are they effective? Do people really hate them? I thought we could pose those and dozens of other questions about commercials.

In my mind the subject was actually about as controversial as a roll of paper towels, but when the word got around that we were about to tackle commercials, one would have thought that CBS News had turned traitor to its own industry. Perhaps it was the record of documentaries gone by that raised the flags of warning. At any rate, we forged ahead and, under Irv Drasnin, fashioned a broadcast of sorts on the subject.

I say "of sorts" because we got little cooperation from the advertising or broadcasting industry, and we were delayed by an unanticipated problem. Obviously, it was appropriate to use samples from many different commercials in our broadcast. But the Screen Actors Guild wanted payment for each and every performer in each and every commercial of the dozens we chose as examples. The negotiations were tense and quite bitter, and we ended up paying a fairly large lump-sum settlement.

The advance furor was a tempest in a teapot. "You and the Commercial" aired on April 26, 1973, and did, I think, perform a modest public service, teaching a few million people a few things about commercials that they hadn't known before.

One of the last broadcasts to come under my aegis before I left the CBS News division provided an extraordinary demonstration of both the power of television and the power of an organized, determined lobby. It was "The Guns of Autumn," also produced by Irv Drasnin.

The best broadcasts do not preach; they simply show. The Murrow-Friendly documentary on McCarthy did spend about a minute at the very end with Ed's famous summation of the case against McCarthy, but the broadcast essentially showed McCarthy in action, letting him reveal himself in his own words. So it was with many other great documentaries. The camera showed what needed to be seen, and the eyes of the viewers were opened.

Such was the case too with "The Guns of Autumn." Scene after graphically filmed scene showed the American hunter at large—tracking deer, bear, wildfowl, even imported big game inside a small preserve. Not a single word of narration was critical of hunters or hunting. But just as a camera roaming almost any battlefield would surely provide raw material for a film that cried out against war, so "The Guns of Autumn" was perceived as a powerful statement against the killing of animals.

Here was another broadcast about which we could be almost certain in advance that there would be protests. In fact, objections started long before the broadcast ever went on the air. Drasnin was a careful and experienced producer, but he had never been through anything like "Project Nassau," "Hunger in America" or "The Selling of the Pentagon." I spent many hours with him trying to make absolutely certain that everything he shot would stand up to scrutiny, that our strict guidelines on staging would be observed to the letter. When all the filming and editing were done, he was as confident as a man could be that there was no way the broadcast could be successfully attacked.

In the months after "The Guns of Autumn" went on the air, the National Rifle Association and other branches of the gun lobby turned their full forces upon us, quite predictably. There was a concerted, organized letter-writing campaign. I personally received more than 30,000 letters and cards, all individually written but most with the same content. I kept getting those cards and letters as long as a year later, and I am sure that Drasnin did also. There were accusations of staging, not to my surprise. If you didn't like what you saw on the tube, it must have been rigged.

In fact, the documentary stood up well against the sound and fury of the lobby against it. No Congressional inquiry was ever mounted, no action ever taken by the FCC. Three lawsuits did, however, grow out of "The Guns of Autumn." Two were dismissed. A jury found CBS News guilty of invading the privacy of a duck hunter in the third suit, and he was awarded a compensatory cash judgment of one dollar.

It is a sad truth that the programs with the longest "half-life" are almost invariably those that rub powerful interests the wrong way, and the resultant opposition to such broadcasts gives them a fame they might not otherwise have achieved. "The Guns of Autumn" was one of these. A solid piece of television journalism, it was one of many CBS News broadcasts through the years to be buffeted by the winds of controversy.

I recall, for instance, two superb miniseries by John Sharnik, "Health in America" and "Justice in America," as well as "The Warren Report—A CBS Inquiry," produced by Les Midgley with a major assist from Bernard Birnbaum. These were major pieces of investigative television journalism, but generally speaking they were heaped with nothing but praise. If a powerful lobby or legislator had gotten the wind up about one of these superb efforts, they would be remembered even today, years after they had served their viewers. Like so many CBS News broadcasts, and so many of the CBS News staffers who fashioned them, they deserved to be.

10

"IT'S YOUR CANDY STORE, MR. PALEY"

I f it is true that we are all bound by the limits of our own generation, I suppose I am bound to a generation raised on the power of the written word. And although I spent most of my working life in radio and television, the old "fundamentals" seem exceedingly important. I would still hire a radio or television reporter on the basis of his or her skill with words on paper.

Walter Cronkite would sometimes propose that *all* CBS News people be hired directly from newspapers, never from local TV or radio. I am of the Walter Cronkite school. Walter, along with a dwindling group who had served on papers, looked around and saw young people on the air who could barely parse a simple sentence; many would have failed a literacy test. As the years rolled on and more and more people watched more and more television news, they seemed to be satisfied with less and less content. At local stations the word "newsperson" often means appropriate looks, age, sex, race and smile.

I was sitting with Eric Sevareid once, when a local newscast came on. "My God, whatever happened to the English language?" he said. Well, whatever happened to it, it certainly does not flourish on local TV. This is not surprising in a trade whose training ground teaches you not to write but to speak.

When I was perhaps twelve years old, my father said to me, "Whatever you do in life, work at least a few years on a newspaper. It is the best training for anything else you might do." He was a lawyer, but he thought newspaper people got to see life, from A through Z, in a way that no office workers ever did.

I followed my father's advice, and never regretted it. When I had children of my own, I passed on the advice. My stepson Chris Wallace thought he might like to go into television news when he got out of college. His father, Mike, and I did everything short of insisting that he work first for a newspaper. Chris saw the wisdom in this, and he actually did spend several years with *The Boston Globe* before he was launched in a television reporting career. When the opportunity for a television job presented itself, Chris was prepared. He could write well, because he had written and written, and he could be an effective reporter, because he had reported and reported. My guess is that if his son Peter ever thinks about going into the television business, Chris will uphold family tradition and say, "Start on a newspaper."

Men with first-class minds do not generally end up in the television news business. All through college and graduate school they have heard the sneers of their professors, who have cautioned them to avoid it. I think this is unfortunate because the single "secret weapon" in television news at the network level is the ability to write well. An astonishing number of key figures at NBC and CBS News (I know ABC less well) are excellent writers, ranging from merely graceful to genuinely talented.

At NBC David Brinkley, John Chancellor and Fred Freed come to mind at once as examples; I have left out several from sheer ignorance. Roger Mudd writes very well. Reuven Frank, too, is a writer. He held many jobs at NBC News, as writer, producer of election convention broadcasts and documentaries, as executive producer of the *Nightly News* and President of the news division. He did them all splendidly, aided by a rainbow connection from mind to paper.

At CBS News, my list of talented writers is much longer, because I have known them so much better. Good television writing is not so much noticed by the viewer as it is felt. An extraordinary synergy takes place when good writing is married to good imagery. The resultant impact is greater than either could be alone. Sometimes it is the words in contrast to the picture that make a point, sometimes a few carefully wrought words underscore a news scene of horror, or of beauty.

Eric Sevareid heads anyone's list of superb writers, not simply because he knows how to write (learning to speak gracefully was a painful process) but because he nearly always has something worth saying. Ed Murrow wrote well, although without the range or the deft touch of a Sevareid. It was Murrow's great organ of a voice that always seemed to stretch an ordinary double into an inside-the-park home run. And Charles Collingwood, a consummate professional in every aspect of the television journalist's trade, wrote so well you never noticed it.

Around CBS News, it did not take long for word about a new boy to get around, especially if he wrote well. "He's a *real* writer" was the highest praise newsmen could confer on a colleague. It was quickly said of Harry Reasoner, and of Charles Kuralt when he was still only in his early twenties. Charles Osgood's deft, light touch—in doggerel, no less—made him famous along the corridors of CBS News. And Bernard Goldberg too has made his mark because he writes so well.

Bob Trout's case is an interesting one. Bob was such a *talker* that I suppose no one ever thought of him as a writer. But the copy he got down on paper was as clean and crisp and smooth as his voice. He was as silky a news reader as I ever came across, and without question the most surefooted of all ad-libbers, radio or television. Bob (now retired and living in Spain) was almost *too* good a broadcaster:

Whether the job of the moment was describing a major catastrophe or just another New Year's Eve in Times Square, his words always flowed without a stumble, perhaps at the expense of feeling. In 1964, when Trout was briefly teamed with Roger Mudd to cover the Democratic Convention, a colleague said, "I don't know if he can replace Cronkite, but he would have been my man at the Resurrection."

I got to know Trout particularly well in those convention days. Even by 1964 standards, Bob was quaintly old-fashioned: a coanchor of advancing years, whose attire bespoke quality Bond Street circa 1938—the best prewar stuff. He would have been uncomfortable if we had urged him to cultivate a more modern look, so we just said to hell with it, let Trout be Trout. We had already had a bit of unforeseen difficulty transporting Bob and his wife, Kit, from New York to San Francisco to the earlier Republican Convention, which he was to anchor for CBS Radio News. The Trouts did not fly. Period. In those days a train trip from New York to San Francisco took more than a week. We could ill afford to spare him for that length of time. But fly? No. The beloved Trouts stood firm. Bill Eames, one of my key deputies at the time, consoled us by saying, "Oh, well, suppose they said they would only take separate trains!"

Bob shunned most travel, much preferring shanks' mare. He and Kit, both string-bean lean, tramped happily through almost every street in Manhattan, marking off the routes they had covered on a large map. His sweet ignorance of the America that lay beyond New York struck me when Kappy and I drove him to Atlantic City for his rendezvous with the television anchor booth of the 1964 Democratic Convention. When we came to the entrance of the New Jersey Thruway and I reached out to snatch the ticket from the toll machine Bob was fascinated. "Good heavens!" he said (it was his strongest expletive). "How long have things like this been going on?"

There is one quality I admire that has really nothing to do with the news business. It comes in people of all shapes and sizes, and you will find it at the top or very near the top of a thousand enterprises large and small. That quality is energy, sustained personal energy over a long period of time. The human internal combustion engine. Combined with a reasonably high level of intelligence plus some innate ambition, it matters little whether an individual ends up in the cement business or television. You could not have kept Mike Wallace or Don Hewitt down on the farm if you had chained them to milking machines. They were born to run. The same was true of Fred Friendly, about whom someone once said, "It's a good thing he wasn't a cigarette salesman; we'd all have had lung cancer."

I would also add Frank Stanton to that list of human dynamos. Neither rain nor hail nor dark of night could keep Stanton from his appointed rounds, running CBS not five but six, often *seven*, days a week. Smart executives knew that if you wanted a quiet talk with Frank you dropped around to his office any Saturday morning—he was sure to be at work. What a lucky thing it was for broadcasting that Frank wrote his doctoral thesis on radio research and landed at CBS. What a lucky thing for CBS News. For that matter, what a lucky thing for William S. Paley.

Stanton was cast in somewhat of a bad-guy role in a docudrama about Ed Murrow. But for my money, if Stanton is a bad guy the moon is made of Brie. For decade after decade he stood firm, a reasoned voice of leadership in the cause of equal rights for broadcast news under the First Amendment, rights still not fully achieved. He testified before Congress scores of times, risking a jail sentence with "The Selling of the Pentagon."

The worth of any news operation is limited by the support it receives from its managers—financial and moral. Year after year, Frank Stanton gave us both. Many at CBS were in awe of him; some feared him. He was quiet, remote, very efficient and liked things around him in perfect order, reflecting the way things were inside his head. I was one of the people who always found him easy to deal with, invariably fair and polite. Stanton has a robust sense of humor, some may be surprised to learn, and I would feel as rewarded by his guffaw or even his wink as by a word of praise. The

Paley-Stanton relationship was something else. It has been described as tense, uneven, yet close. Perhaps, over the years, it was all three. My observation, sitting well below the salt, was that Frank seemed to handle Paley in much the way a wily prime minister would deal with an equally shrewd, erratic—but absolute—monarch.

Stanton could be a problem. He noticed too much. Let a graphic be out of place or a bit of audio distorted and he spotted it fast. He seemed to have several sets of eyes and ears, all tuned. We were proud of our election set, which was invariably complicated and expensive to rig up, and so I would ask Frank to come over to have a look before the big night. He would always find something out of place. If there was nothing wrong, he'd seem fretful anyway. One year, my deputy, Bob Wussler, suggested we beat Frank to the punch. On the roster of states we decided to spell *Kansas* incorrectly, to see if he'd spot it. He did. "*Kansus*—I bet you did that on purpose," he said, laughing.

Everyone at CBS in the Stanton days had favorite Stanton stories. Not a few concerned Black Rock, the remarkable building at 51 West 52nd Street that will be known forever among CBS people as Stanton's building. Almost everything about it, right down to whether the restroom doors would say M and W or MEN and WOMEN, was his creation, though its official architect was Eero Saarinen. At first even the art in individual offices was selected and hung only on the say-so of top CBS brass, frequently Frank Stanton himself.

One Saturday morning in 1966, when CBS was still at 485 Madison, Stanton had the unpleasant duty of telling James Aubrey, President of the CBS Television Network, that he was fired. Aubrey was astonished. True, he had been getting a bushel of bad publicity that reflected not only on his own image but on that of CBS. But fired? There must be some mistake. He protested that he had done everything asked of him. The network was riding high, profits at their peak.

Aubrey demanded to see Paley. The Chairman was ill, Stanton

told him, confined to bed in a nearby hotel with a painful back condition. Aubrey insisted on seeing him anyway. Stanton made the call to Paley. "He'll see you right away. Go right over."

A distraught Aubrey hurried from the office, and Stanton, as usual virtually alone in the building on a Saturday morning, busied himself with a pile of papers. About forty minutes later the phone rang. It was Paley. "I thought you told me Aubrey was coming over."

"You mean he hasn't shown up?"

"That's right."

"I can't understand it. It's a five-minute walk. I'll check his office. Call me the minute he comes."

Stanton felt first faintly then increasingly apprehensive. He walked down a flight to Aubrey's office. It was empty. He phoned down to the elevator guard station and spoke to the man on duty.

"Have you seen Mr. Aubrey?"

"Saw him when he came in."

"Did you see him leave?"

"No, sir."

"Are you sure?"

"Yes, sir. If he had gone out, I'd have seen him."

Stanton checked the men's room, then Aubrey's office again. He kept telling himself not to worry. Aubrey was too cool a customer. Aubrey could dish it out, so he probably could take it. Nevertheless, Stanton opened a window and took a fast look at the street down below. Relief. His view was restricted, though, so he rode down to the lobby and walked around the full perimeter of the building. Nothing. He returned to his office and called the Chairman. Aubrey had not shown.

For another half hour Stanton brooded at his desk, his head in his hands. He was ready to call the police. At last the phone rang. Paley was on the line.

"Aubrey's here. He told me he walked out of the building and went for a long walk over by the East River to get hold of himself before he came up here . . . Frank? Are you all right, Frank?"

No one in the news division wept when Aubrey left. The expenses we incurred, the air time we occupied, the ratings we didn't get—all stood in the way of the mission he was determined to fulfill, to make more money for the CBS Television Network than had ever been made before. In 1964, he walked into our set at the GOP National Convention in San Francisco, took one look around, muttered, "Waste of money"—and strode out. It was hardly encouraging to the CBS News team on the eve of a convention. Jack Schneider, Gene Jankowski, Jim Rosenfield would never have said such a thing, even if they had thought it.

There were a number of years when Stanton was a more visible presence and perhaps more the embodiment of "CBS power" even than Chairman Paley. All of us then in the news division remember the days following the assassination of John F. Kennedy. As a correspondent with assignments in New York and Washington, I was part of a magnificent effort by all people at all of the networks. I recall those days to relate a small incident that underscores the pervasiveness of that kind of power and how it rolls on, at times far beyond the intention of those who wield it.

On the third day of CBS's coverage of the assassination, our exhausted troops in the anchor area above Grand Central Terminal needed a boost. Someone suggested that Stanton himself come around for a short encouraging visit. Of course he did so, heaping quiet words of praise on Ernie Leiser, who was in charge of our coverage, director Don Hewitt, the indefatigable Walter Cronkite and all those present. In the course of his visit, however, Stanton was heard to murmur (to no one in particular, but apparently within range of one of the several minions in his visiting party), "This place could certainly use a coat of paint."

The next morning an exhausted Hewitt dragged himself into the anchor area to prepare to direct coverage of the funeral day. He was aghast to find the place swarming with workmen wielding paint buckets, ladders—all kinds of paraphernalia that can get in the way of broadcasting.

"What the fuck is going on here?" he screamed.

"Dr. Stanton's orders," said one of the men. "Sorry."

The exact routing of the next couple of phone calls is not recorded. Needless to say, the painters and their brushes were out of there before Hewitt and Leiser tore them apart with their bare hands.

Coverage of the Kennedy tragedy was called television's finest hour. Perhaps it was, although since that time there have been other times, sometimes again in the wake of national tragedy, when the networks brought the nation together in common mourning or shared pride—from the assassinations of Bobby Kennedy and Martin Luther King, Jr., to the triumph of the moon walk. The public today accepts the ability of the networks—their technicians and their news people—to handle such events. I venture to say that only our training in political convention coverage, two intense weeks every four years beginning as early as 1948, could have given us the capability of rising to those sad or splendid occasions.

Paley and Stanton played one-two in another famous now-you-see-him-now-you-don't CBS story. A nice guy named Tom Dawson, avid golfer, crack salesman, found himself President of the CBS Television Network at one point. Following the departure of Jim Aubrey, the job was nothing if not insecure, but Tom did well at it, or so he thought, until one day, after a year or so, Stanton called him in and lowered the boom. Like Aubrey before him, Tom couldn't believe it. Here he was, not fifty years old, and they were cutting off his career. He asked to see Paley. Okay.

This time no sneaking out, no long walk. Just into the Chairman's office.

"I certainly accept your judgment, yours and Frank's," Dawson began. "I just wonder, before I go, whether you would be good enough to give me a *reason*."

Bill Paley, some twenty years Dawson's senior, flung his arm with real affection around his shoulder. "Tom," he said, with a note of sadness, "we just *have* to make room for *younger* men."

Dawson capitulated. "It's your candy store, Mr. Paley." A phrase that gained a certain vogue among those who thought it would be forever true.

11

LIFE
ON THE
WASHINGTON
MERRY-GO-AROUND

One day in October 1975 I was at a news panel conference at Harvard when Arthur Taylor, then President of CBS, phoned me. A call from him was not in itself unusual, in spite of the several layers of bureaucracy separating us, but the fact that the call drew me out of a meeting meant something was up. Would I please see him as soon as I returned to New York?

Arthur Taylor was, at that time, Paley's hand-picked choice to succeed him. In his mid-thirties, handsome and confident, with an intellectual bent and a reputation for financial brilliance, Taylor took his work and his life very, very seriously.

During his first months at CBS, he learned quickly that CBS News was not simply another commodity that could be measured entirely by the bottom line but an asset (occasionally a liability) to be nurtured, protected and defended. He had come to be an enthusiastic supporter of CBS News and put his full weight behind a drive to persuade the CBS affiliates to accept an hour-long evening news broadcast, although his efforts proved unsuccessful.

The 35th floor of the CBS building is where God would have had his office if they had made room for him, the late Bob Wood once said to me, when he was President of the CBS Television Network. CBS's stand-in for the Almighty, William S. Paley, occupies the northeast corner of the floor; his suite includes not only an office but a reception room, dining room, kitchen and secretarial area. In a building that is mostly Stanton and where everything "fits" precisely, Paley's office is extraordinary: It is all Paley, a marvelously put together hodgepodge that includes an old chemin de fer table, a big Eames chair and clusters of old-time radio microphones scattered among the books and other bibelots. The off-white walls boast paintings and drawings that open wide a visitor's eyes—Rouault, Derain, Ben Nicholson, a big abstract by his friend Picasso. The Paley office is a liveable museum piece.

In the northwest corner of the floor is the presidential suite to which I repaired for my meeting with Arthur Taylor. To get there I had walked down corridors of carpet as rich as the men who worked here. A few offices ring the southern exposure, for lesser corporate lights, and there is an elaborate boardroom protecting the western flank, but the doors to all these are kept discreetly closed. Almost no sound disturbs the 35th floor. A visitor, stepping off an elevator and spotting the reception area between the Chairman's and the President's suites, might wonder what if anything goes on in these offices. Ironically, for a business in which speech and communication are primary, silence seems the only commodity up for sale here.

I was afraid Arthur Taylor would say, "It was good of you to come over on such short notice." Smooth executives are forever in the habit of saying things to subordinates like "Don't let me inconvenience you" or "If you have a moment," euphemisms for "Drop everything, I want you now," but he got right down to cases. "How would you like to go to Washington and work for me there?" he asked.

I knew immediately the job he was talking about: CBS's chief lobbyist with Congress, the Federal Communications Commission, the White House—its major interests in Washington. I had heard that Richard Jencks, former head of the CBS Broadcast Group, who had been playing this role, was leaving the company.

"Arthur," I said, "I don't know anything about lobbying. I don't know anything about the problems you have there. All I know about is news."

"Half the problems the networks have in Washington are news problems," he said. "As far as the rest of the stuff is concerned, you're not too old to learn, and you've been around the company for years—you really know it inside and out, if you think about it. Besides, I want to take a personal interest in Washington and I'd like to have someone there whom I know and trust and can work with."

I told Taylor that I would think about it, and I did just that, talking first to my wife. "It sounds exciting," Kappy said. "I'd like to live in Washington. But what is it that you would do?"

"I'm not really sure. Lobby, I guess."

"Is that dirty?"

"I don't think so. It's what lawyers do. They put their client's case in the best possible light. This would be CBS."

"Well, you love CBS."

"More or less."

"Well, we ought to do it," she said emphatically.

I talked to Dick Salant, who seemed surprised that I would even consider Taylor's offer. "Why would you want to do a thing like that?" he snapped. A statement more than a question.

"I don't know."

But I did know. Through thick and thin with Salant, Friendly, then Salant again, I had been close to—but not quite at the top of—CBS News for more than a dozen years. I was fifty-nine years old. I could look forward to five or six more years before retirement, the last several of which I would serve under Bill Small, who had been brought up from Washington first to succeed Gordon Manning to run hard news and ultimately to replace Salant as President of News, when Dick retired.

Curiously enough, I had never yearned to be President of News. I had worked so closely with Friendly and Salant that I felt actually being President would offer me very little beyond what I already had. Bill Small and I worked reasonably well together (although not nearly as closely as Gordon Manning and I had); I couldn't help wondering what it might be like, down the line, working for Bill in my twilight years. Possibly it would be fine. But here was a chance to face a new challenge, undoubtedly the last of my career, and to meet new faces in a new town. I speculated that if I really hated the Washington job, CBS News would find some useful work for a loyal though aging manager, correspondent or producer, but I didn't mull things over for long.

I called up Arthur Taylor and told him I would take the job.

"That's terrific," he said. "You'll report to me, but on a day-to-day basis, of course, you'll work through Kidder Meade here in New York." Meade and I were old friends. He was head of corporate relations at CBS, which meant he operated with three sometimes conflicting priorities. The first was to make Chairman Paley look good. The second and third, more or less on a par, were to make the President, Arthur Taylor, and the entire corporation look good. Meade was a stocky man with what must have been, years before, a baby face. Now it showed the strain of the no-man's-land he inhabited, caught between the Scylla of the imperial lifelong Chairman and the Charybdis of whoever was President.

Kidder Meade was a West Pointer (he had lost a leg in World War II), and he seemed to have transferred some of the come-hell-or-high-water dedication that marks the professional soldier to the cause of CBS. His devotion to the company was intense, and there was no trick of the persuader's art he would not employ. He was a plotter, happy to operate behind the scenes, and for years one of the shadowy, powerful figures at CBS. The wrong side of Kidder Meade was a dangerous place to find oneself on.

I sat now in his small office on the 35th floor. As we talked, his secretary walked in and put a small piece of folded white paper on his desk. He smiled, unfolded it and pushed it toward me.

"Here," he said. "Read that."

The paper read 38½.

"That's the price of CBS stock at noon. That's the bottom line. You're not in the news business anymore."

"I see." I must have looked a little puzzled.

"Don't get me wrong, CBS is more than just dollars and cents. Paley knows that. Stanton most certainly did. He knew how important Washington is to this company. Arthur would like Washington to think of him the way they used to think of Frank Stanton."

"Just like that."

"Well, he *sees* himself moving in that direction. Arthur *likes* all that Washington business. Once you get to know the ropes, you're going to have to show him off down there. He's the President of CBS, and it shows we care and still believe in the same thing Stanton believed in."

"Do we?"

"Sure we do."

"I'm glad to hear that."

And so we went to Washington.

I think I learned more about how government really works in my few short years as a Washington lobbyist than in all my years as a reporter, though that may say more for my inadequacies as a journalist than it does for the lessons to be learned marching through the halls of Congress, sitting in a hearing room or sipping bourbon in the office of the gentleman from West Virginia.

Lobbyists. Of course, we are all lobbyists, selling the interest of the group or unit for which we are responsible, whether we are paid or not. And regardless of other talents or qualities that got them their jobs, all corporate chief executives spend much if not most of their time lobbying on behalf of their companies. Ronald Reagan may be the finest lobbyist in recent American history.

Still, lobbying—selling a point of view—does not come easily to a newspaperman, in whose very bones is the conviction that the proper role of news and news people is not to *sell* but to *report*, to get at the truth as best one can and to pass it on. At CBS News the role of lobbyist was to sell and defend the efficacy of that simple but infinitely difficult role.

The news division has a very large Washington office—a whole building in fact, by far the largest of all the CBS "foreign" bureaus. About two hundred correspondents, producers, technicians and managers work there. I knew it almost as well as our offices in New York. It was from 2020 M Street, as a correspondent, that I had been sent out on assignments covering the Kennedy funeral, and it was there that I had flown to supervise the last hours of our coverage of the Nixon resignation. For years I had been aware that in a corner of that building a respected former CBS News executive, Ted Koop, ran what was vaguely referred to as the "corporate office." No one seemed to know exactly what Ted did, and news people did not seem to care. Then, at about the time Ted Koop retired, what was deemed the impropriety of mixing news space and lobbying space resulted in the establishment of new quarters down the block, grander quarters, for CBS Inc., and that is where I landed.

Until the Reagan administration came along, broadcasters, who belong to one of the most regulated of all industries, were always hanging close to the edge of a cliff, afraid that some combination of sons of bitches in Washington was aut to strangle their golden goose. In the late 1970s nearly three hundred people were employed in Washington by the broadcasting and cable interests, looking after their particular causes and in some cases fighting each other. The National Association of Broadcasters has a good-looking building at the corner of 18th and N Streets that would put to shame most of the embassies in town. It had, and still has, teams of researchers, lawyers, Capitol Hill lobbyists and FCC specialists. The NAB, financed by television and radio broadcasters around the country, can organize—and on occasion has organized—enormous grass-roots pressure on legislators.

It is true that in theory the FCC and Congress control broadcasters, and can shut them down, although it is virtually unheard of. The other side of the coin is that broadcasters control the airwaves and, theoretically, might make it harder or easier for a candidate to get air time. Editorial endorsement is the least subtle way that a local broadcaster can flex his political muscle. One of the first things I learned in Washington was that no one has more immediate access to Senator A or Congressman B than the owner or manager of the hometown station. Each of the major networks has Washington offices—definitely a growth industry since the days when Ted Koop ran a one- or two-man shop.

I inherited an attractive and able young assistant named Rae Evans, who made it clear that my first task was to pay personal calls on all the people in Washington who were important to CBS. These included each member of the FCC, the chairmen of the Senate Commerce Committee and its Communications Subcommittees and their counterparts in the House. "Those are the people who *count*, as far as we're concerned," Rae stated emphatically. "Except on special issues like, say, copyright you can throw the rest of them away. I don't mean that literally, you understand."

I told her I understood, but the truth is that at the time I did not. Gradually, however, I came to realize that we moved in a very tight little orbit in the larger world of government and politics.

Dutifully I made my calls, first alone, later with Arthur Taylor, who, true to his word, flung himself early and often upon the Washington scene. People such as Richard Wiley, Chairman of the FCC, and Lionel Van Deerlin, Chairman of the House Communications Subcommittee, became acquaintances and finally our good friends.

I had not been in Washington very long before I realized that my doubts about leaving New York and News were vanishing. Part of that was due to personal good fortune. Thanks to Arthur Taylor and his assistant, Kathryn Pelgrift, Kappy and I were able to arrange the financing of a beautiful home. Arthur said he thought it was the kind of a place CBS's Washington representative ought to live in.

We liked that attitude, and we were pleased whenever he came down from New York and spent the night with us.

Shortly after we arrived in Washington, CBS gave a very large welcoming party for us, and in a stroke we were launched into the business and social whirl of the nation's capital. Almost immediately Kappy and I began to make new friends. I was quite busy, but the endless pressures of New York were gone.

Our Washington office was expanding. In addition to Rae Evans, two other able young people, Jack Loftus and Roger Colloff, were working with me. Both knew a good deal about the Washington game, enough to keep me out of trouble, into which I surely would have drifted had I staggered about on my own. From their CBS Washington jobs, all three have moved on smartly. Colloff later returned to New York with me, becoming a CBS News Vice President and ultimately General Manager of WCBS-TV.

The issues we dealt with ranged from the mildly boring, such as CBS interests in a new copyright law, to those I considered of fundamental importance, especially the rights of broadcasting under the First Amendment, for which we had fought with only indifferent success over the years. I discovered what many had before me, that there are dozens of ways to lobby but nothing beats having a good case to start with, hard work and a desire to help the other guy.

Of all the great American corporations, CBS was arguably the most visible and the most controversial on Capitol Hill during my stint in Washington. As an extremely successful network, we commanded a respect tinged with envy and suspicion. All day and all night, every day and every night, CBS had the capacity to reach millions of Americans, as no legislator could come close to doing. CBS symbolized the power—to many, the dangerous power—of the networks. Only a few years earlier, the House had come very close to citing Frank Stanton for contempt of Congress in the "Selling of the Pentagon" case. CBS News was at the core of the love-hate relationship the network had with Congress, the White House and the FCC.

On the one hand, there was general recognition of CBS News's fierce independence, the quality of its product and its service to the public, particularly at times of national emergency. Perhaps above all, there was Walter Cronkite, who was much respected in Washington. On the other hand, like *The New York Times* and *The Washington Post*, CBS News seemed constantly to be against whatever administration was in power. Inevitably, elements in any administration, any legislature, saw network television news people as liberals at best, "Commies" at worst. Looking at the dark side, then, CBS smelled too rich, too strong and sometimes damn well un-American.

So I was somewhat surprised at how friendly everyone seemed. For years I had casually read of CBS squabbles with the FCC, threatening speeches in House and Senate, ugly resolutions, some of them aimed at network news. Only occasionally did a favorable word on one of our broadcasts appear in the *Congressional Record*. I expected an aloof, if not downright hostile, environment. But I was welcomed, almost as if I had joined a club.

All those concerned with communications legislation and regulation—congressmen, commissioners, committee staff members, lawyers—labored in the same special vineyard. They were lobbyists all, bound by their mutual interests and their tensions, and when work was done they tended to play together. Some of the good times were underwritten by the networks, though seldom were they anything more lavish than individual lunches or dinners. Once a year Peter Kenney, the NBC man in town, hosted a large cocktail buffet that overflowed his home and at which one could find all the good old boys from House, Senate and FCC. Richard Jencks, an ardent tennis player, got the bright idea of a CBS celebrity tennis tournament—a super-lobby—at which nary a word of business would be permitted. It still takes place annually in Washington, and invitations to play are much coveted among the tennis set, cabinet level included.

Despite the pleasure of new friends and my gratitude that I was still able to make a contribution to the success of the company I loved, my stint in Washington was long on routine and short on excitement. A favorable phrase added to the wording of a bill that in itself would probably never be passed into law might be the heart-warming result of two weeks of friendly persuasion.

I never heard of money changing hands in an exchange for a vote or a favor in the communications business in Washington. The communications business, like every other business, supports the elected officials who deal with legislation that can affect them. In the case of broadcasters, it means particularly cooperating with the Communications Subcommittees of the House and Senate Commerce Committees and their staffs. Members of the FCC are not elected, but they have their constituency, and the networks are an important element. I got to know all of the commissioners well. They varied in intelligence, but all were serious about their work, trying hard to be fair.

One day in 1977, Kidder Meade called me from New York. "Are you sitting down?" A serious opening gambit.

"Go ahead, Kidder."

"Paley fired Taylor. John Backe is the new President."

I received this as a staggering piece of news. I had seen Arthur frequently since I took the Washington job and had become part of his small coterie. I made one or two trips a week to New York to confer with him or Meade, and Taylor seldom let a month go by without flying down to Washington for a Congressional or FCC call. I had heard him complain about Paley. "That old man," he would say, shaking his head. "I don't know what to do about him."

"My God, Kidder," I said, "what the hell happened?"

"He just called him into his office before the Board meetings and said he'd decided to make a change and that was that. Period," Meade said. "Well, here we go again."

John Backe, then head of the CBS Publishing Group, a comparatively small part of the CBS empire, is a quiet, serious man of medium just-about-everything. The wisecrack making the rounds the day after the surprise announcement was that Backe happened to be on the 35th floor after Taylor's firing and was the first person Paley saw and recognized. He was, in fact, an extremely decent fellow who did the very best he could under trying circumstances.

Backe was an insider, succeeding two outsiders as President. But he was an insider only in the sense that he was a CBS employee. Because he had no broadcasting or even record industry experience, he knew few people in our core businesses, and none of them were his people. Still, his only real problem turned out to be the one that mattered most: William S. Paley.

When he was President, John Backe had little knowledge of, or interest in, CBS's Washington problems. Dutifully he made the rounds of the House and Senate bigwigs with me and met one or two members of the FCC. He seemed perpetually to be gritting his even, white teeth, and with obvious relief he'd get back on the company plane and head for the more familiar shores of New York.

Less than three years later, I saw Backe in Los Angeles, where he was addressing the annual conference of CBS affiliates at the Century Plaza Hotel. I knew he had come out on one of the company planes and, as usual, he must be eager to go back to New York. So was I, and I asked him if I could bum a ride. He told me to be at the airport promptly at 7:00 A.M. We rode alone in the luxurious Gulfstream II, television land far below us, and chatted most of the way. He asked me what I planned to do and where I thought I would live when I retired, and he told me about the orange groves in which he had invested. It was a mellow interlude.

The trip seemed to take no time at all, although by the clock it was just after lunchtime in New York when we landed at La Guardia. John Backe's limousine was there to meet him. So was mine.

I thanked him for the plane ride and said, "I'll be seeing you."

A little later that afternoon Backe walked into Bill Paley's office and Paley told him he was through. Before the end of the day he had left the CBS building, never to return. I have not seen him since we parted at the airport and he headed, unwittingly, for the guillotine. If ever there was a man who seemed untroubled by the immediate future, it was John Backe on his last trip in a CBS plane.

Early in 1978, I began to hear reports that Bill Small, Executive Vice President of CBS News, might not succeed Dick Salant as planned. Eric Sevareid, an old friend of mine and originally a big booster of Small's for the job of President of CBS News, was one of the first to mention this to me. Kidder Meade was another. Meade told me over the course of almost a year that he thought I deserved the job and should have it. I said I appreciated his sweet thought but I was past sixty and had no desire to be a caretaker.

For several months, each time I came to New York Meade would bring the subject up again. He had no direct power, of course, but I knew he had Paley's ear. He liked Bill Small and had known him for a long time, but when he seemed to confirm the rumors going around that Bill had somehow just missed the boat, I began to take him seriously. I mentioned all this one night to Kappy. "How would you feel about it if I was asked to go back to New York and run CBS News?"

"I think it would be ridiculous," she said. "Promise me you won't do a thing like that. It's a terrible job. You're much too old. We've never been as happy as we are right here."

"I haven't been asked. It was just something Kidder talked about."

Kappy gave me a look that said, If by chance it should happen, I know there'd be no stopping you.

A few weeks later, at a party to celebrate the tenth anniversary of 60 Minutes at the Four Seasons restaurant in New York, John Backe drew me into a quiet corner. "I'd like you to come by my office tomorrow. I want to talk to you about coming back to New York to succeed Dick Salant as President of CBS News."

I knew that my short career as a Washington lobbyist was over. And, somewhat to my surprise, I realized that I was excited. Was it the challenge that lay ahead? A chance to see how I would handle a job I had observed so closely for so long? Not entirely. Most of all, I realized how much I had missed the New York scene and the CBS people I had worked with, played with, often fought with, some of them for more than three decades. Rarely did I enter the lobby of 524 West 57th without a half glance at the plaque honoring Murrow and the thought that this was his place, that he was the reason we were here.

I was going back. To that place and to those people.

12

RUNNING
CBS NEWS

———

Although it was John Backe who had first approached me about running CBS News, I knew that if I did accept the job my direct boss would be Gene Jankowski, head of the CBS Broadcast Group. One day in spring 1978, Gene called me in Washington to ask whether I would be going to the meeting of the European Broadcasting Union to be held in Athens the last weekend in June. I told him I was. "That's great," he said. "Actually, I'm bringing the family, but they can all go sightseeing one morning or afternoon while we have a little talk."

Quite the most engaging spot in Athens, unless you insist on being in the heart of downtown, is the Astir Palace Hotel, a long taxi ride from the Parthenon, but quiet and luxurious. Gene and I sat in a shaded garden and discussed my future.

"First," he said, "let me ask you something. Would you have any problem working for me?"

"No, of course not. Why should I have?"

I could see Gene was almost blushing. "Well," he said, "you know, when I first knew you, you were already sort of, well, established, on the air, and I was just a kid salesman . . . and I thought perhaps . . ." He left the sentence trailing in the pine-scented Greek air.

"Oh," I said, the truth dawning on me, "because you're so much *younger*."

Gene looked relieved. He was, in fact, more than twenty years younger.

"I won't give it a second thought." I said.

"That's good," said Gene.

"Which brings *me* to say something. I think I know how you're going to answer, Gene, but I have to say it anyway. I'm not taking this job just to keep the seat warm. It's not my nature. Even if I haven't got much time."

Gene reached over to pat me lightly on the arm. "Of course not. I don't mean, of course, you don't have time—I mean I wouldn't have given you this job if I thought you were going to just sit it out."

"One other thing," I said, "before we go any further. Why now? Salant isn't scheduled to retire until after the first of the year, something like nine months from now."

Gene seemed surprised that I had asked so obvious a question. "Why, you know the answer to that one. The papers are after us day after day. Well, you're in Washington . . . maybe you don't feel the full heat of it. Morale in the news division is really being affected. Who's going to succeed Salant? Small won't make it, but then what? It's gotten to the point where we are all agreed that the thing to do is make the announcement, get the speculation out of the way and give you the job reasonably soon."

"Wait a minute, Gene. I don't think I quite get this. Make the announcement, get the speculation out of the way and give me the job reasonably soon. What does 'reasonably soon' mean? You don't mean go back down to Washington and sit on my ass until Salant retires, do you? That wouldn't make any sense!"

"No, I don't mean that, you would be the Executive Vice President and Chief Operating Officer."

"What exactly would that mean?"

"Well, it would mean that you would be in charge on a day-to-day basis. Keep Dick informed."

"Gene, does Dick know about this?"

"Well, of course he *will* know. When everything is set."

"And how do you think Dick is going to *like* that, somebody else running his candy store while he's still behind the counter?"

"It'll work out," Gene assured me. "You can handle it. I know you can." Dreaded words: If your boss says he knows you can handle it, he has just washed his hands of the whole business. And *you've* got a problem.

At CBS, as at most other companies, a man reaching mandatory retirement at the age of sixty-five has traditionally accepted the milestone with good grace, often relief—delighted, for the moment at least, that he had made it and could rest on his pension. The very highest order of executives, if they were healthy, knew that they were being pushed aside not so much because they could no longer do the job but because they blocked the upward march of ambitious younger men. Nevertheless, they could not help but feel rejected, almost as if they were being fired, when their turn came.

CBS retirement policy did not apply to William S. Paley, the Chairman himself decided, but he invoked it in the case of Frank Stanton. In spite of the honors heaped on Frank at the time, it must have been a galling experience to be put out to pasture.

Dick Salant, I suspected, might feel similarly. By announcing his successor far in advance and putting him right to work, it appeared the company he had served with such distinction for so long could hardly wait to wave him good-bye. I was acutely conscious, therefore, when Jankowski offered me Salant's job that Dick might be resentful about the way he was being treated, and that some of that resentment might be centered on me.

I pledged to myself that I would do everything in my power to make the awkward arrangement as graceful as possible. I hope I did. Dick and I never talked about it then or since, but I am sure he hated every minute of the time he was there during those trying months of transition.

Although Salant went to NBC for a few years after his departure, his love affair with CBS News never ceased. "How is it over there?" a friend would ask, meaning NBC. "It's *awful!*" Salant could hardly wait to shout.

"Now," Jankowski said to me in Athens, "have you thought about what you want to do with CBS News?"

I had. But, to be honest about it, in my years at CBS News I had spent almost all of my time trying to win the battles while higher authorities worried about winning the war. For the past two years in Washington, however, although removed from the fray, I had begun to develop a broader, more strategic view. I had also developed some perspective on the role I felt the news division ought to play in the overall company scheme.

"This is the way I see it," I replied. "I think perhaps the most important thing we can try to do in the next two or three years is to get ready for the future. That's number one. CBS News is best. We're on top. But the upper layer is . . . well . . . getting along in years, they're a generation older than you are, Gene. You can start with Walter, I suppose, Sevareid, Bud Benjamin, Salant, me, Ernie Leiser . . . I could go on. So many of the people who meant so much, who still do mean so much, are reaching retirement age. So I'd say a most important priority is identifying and putting in place the next generation of people who are going to take CBS News into the future."

"Okay," said Gene, "what else?"

"Well, this won't surprise you. One more try for a one-hour news. I know you want it, God knows I want it. Maybe this time we can swing it."

Salant and Cronkite were highly vocal advocates of this idea.

Twice in the past the CBS Television Network had tried to persuade its affiliates to accept a longer *Evening News;* twice a majority of the CBS stations had rejected the proposal. Both times there had been several reasons for the rejection, but most important was that a longer network news would cut into net revenues and reduce local news coverage at a critical time in the early evening. The two other networks had had no better luck than we in persuading their stations to try an hour or even forty-five minutes of evening news.

I had a few other items on my short list. A revitalized morning news program; a prime-time science series starring Walter Cronkite (we called it *Universe* and it ran for a couple of years with very modest success). "And I've got a little Sunday idea we've been thinking about for a long time, Gene."

"Well," said Gene, safe in the armor of his optimism. "Everything looks *great.* I can see you've given it a lot of thought."

So much so that on my shopping list there had been no mention of what quickly became the number-one priority, a replacement for Cronkite on the *CBS Evening News.*

Gene Jankowski acted without delay. On July 14, 1978, I was made Executive Vice President and Chief Operating Officer of CBS News and named specifically to succeed Dick Salant upon his retirement the following spring. I moved immediately into a windowless cubbyhole of an office just to the left of the entrance to the West 57th Street building. To the right of the entrance was the President's office, occupied by Salant, and down the hall just beyond it the office of the number-two man at CBS News, he who had come so very close to the job that would be mine, a colleague and friend of many years, William J. Small.

He was my first assignment. Self-imposed. I had to fire him.

Bill Small was used to virtually running CBS News. Particularly on the hard-news side, people jumped to his tune. I reasoned that if Bill were left in place, whatever discord had resulted in his having been passed over for the presidency would remain, morale would continue to be low, nothing would have changed except that I would have replaced Salant at the top of the pile. I told Gene

Jankowski what I intended to do, and why. "Your call," he said. But then he added, "Bill's a good man. I hope we can find something for him."

It was Kidder Meade—Vice President of Corporate Affairs and a firm friend of Small's—who later found the rather neat, if temporary, solution of having Bill fill the corporate lobbying job in Washington that I had just left. Small accepted it, perhaps with some misgivings, for he had been a newsman all his life. Less than a year later he was chosen to be head of NBC News, and for a while we were competing fiercely against each other, after having worked side by side for so many years. In spite of all this, our personal relationship never soured.

Like Salant, Bill Small could not get CBS News out of his system. When he went over to NBC News, he apparently perceived a major problem with the place: There were not enough people from CBS News to make it work right. And he lured some CBS newsmen over to his new stomping ground. Accordingly, what became known as the CBS Mafia infested NBC News for a while, and this caused some rather serious morale problems. NBC News had a proud tradition, too, after all, and those who had helped to build it over the years resented the notion that the only good television news people came from CBS.

Still, there *was* something about CBS News and CBS News people . . . there were so *many* talented journalists in our shop. And it seemed as if there always had been, going all the way back to the days of Ed Murrow and company. Indeed, that fact caused one of the most serious and time-consuming problems that I faced throughout my years as head of News. For not only Bill Small but also the aggressive Roone Arledge—stimulated by the peripatetic talent agent Richard Leibner—came to believe that a shortcut to upgrading their own operations was simply to raid our staff.

Occasional skipping about from one network to another had always been part of the game, and at the top level it was well publicized: Harry Reasoner to ABC News; Harry Reasoner back to CBS. But there had been surprisingly little high-level raiding over the years. This changed when Arledge came on the scene. When ABC began actively recruiting CBS people—not simply top correspondents but the best producers, too—the kind of money dangled in front of our people was, in a number of cases, simply too much to resist. Though many good workers remained loyal to CBS, they began to feel uneasy living with the tales of how some old colleagues had jumped ship for two, even three times as much money as they had been making at CBS. Our battles to keep the staff of CBS News more or less intact persisted all through 1979, 1980 and 1981.

Richard Leibner, who represented a great many news people, obviously recognized the opportunities, as did one or two other agents. Suddenly all, or very nearly all, CBS News people were worth more. Correspondents Hughes Rudd, Barry Serafin, Betsy Aaron, Jed Duvall and Richard Threlkeld went to ABC, attracted not solely by money but by what they perceived as greater career opportunities. Another serious loss was producer Rick Kaplan.

Perhaps the most publicized of the defections involved the Kalb brothers, Marvin and Bernard, who were sought for NBC News by their old boss, Bill Small. The negotiations to keep them at CBS News centered around Marvin, whose contract had expired. Marvin announced that it was not simply a matter of money (naturally, he wanted his salary doubled); there were two further considerations: First, he wanted his own contract accompanied by a new contract for his brother. More important, he insisted that he appear on the *CBS Evening News* a specific number of times each week and that this be written into his contract. To give in to such a demand would have meant putting part of the editorial control of the evening broadcast in the hands of someone who was not responsible for it. We were genuinely sorry to lose Marvin and Bernie, both of whom made very real contributions to CBS News over many years. If I or one of my colleagues had been a little shrewder, perhaps we could have devised some wording that would have kept both our principles and Marvin's ego intact, but maybe he was hell-bent on joining Bill Small at any cost—even if it made him rich.

Our most successful negotiations, as well as the most expensive, caused hardly a stir. They involved people we felt we had to keep if it was at all possible to do so, and we did. I can recall two cases—though not quite in the class with the Dan Rather bidding battle—in which we simply would not let ABC or NBC money take away people we truly valued. One was Ray Brady, the other Charles Osgood. Brady was recognized as the top network business correspondent at a time when interest in business news was escalating. ABC was willing to more than double his salary if he would work for them when his contract expired. I was determined not to let him go. We paid the price, whatever was necessary to keep him. No principles involved, only money.

Osgood was desperately important to the radio network—and still is. He is one of the few people who give it identity. And, remarkably, he is the only CBS News correspondent who earns a great deal of money because of what he does on radio rather than on television.

Which brings me to Bill Moyers.

When I became President of CBS News in 1978, I did not know Moyers well personally. He had come to CBS News and gone in the brief period that I had spent in Washington. But in that time he had done some extraordinary work, including a remarkably powerful documentary called "The Fire Next Door." I could never quite get a straight story on what there was about CBS News that made him leave, after so short a stay, and go to PBS. I did hear that he was not entirely happy in his new work, which seemed to be about par for the Moyers course. But I knew that I wanted him back.

When I took it over, it seemed to me that CBS News was in danger of losing its soul. The days of Murrow were long past, to say nothing of Howard K. Smith. Sevareid was retiring. Cronkite was past the finish line. The division had many splendid younger people, but I did not have the feeling there were many among them burning with a clear blue flame. Moyers, I knew, was a man who had something to say, and who knew how to say it. He would give the *CBS Evening News* presence, as Sevareid once had. It seemed to me particularly important to have some interesting, even provocative news analysis on the *Evening News* as a counterbalance to Dan Rather's reportorial style.

In 1980 I consulted Howard Stringer, a young executive producer, and Skee Wolff, who knew Moyers best. Both thought the chances of getting him back were only fair, but why not try? Try I did.

A few months later I told a colleague I was getting along beautifully with Bill Moyers.

"Which one?" he quipped.

I was lucky enough to see only one side of Bill Moyers—charming, concerned, interested, thoughtful. In the course of our painfully protracted negotiations, however, most often conducted through parties of the third and sometimes even the fourth part, I *felt* some of the other aspects of Bill Moyers—indecisive, vacillating, coy. Perhaps cunning; one never quite knew.

Finally, in 1981, he agreed to come back to CBS News, where he made an enormous contribution during this five-year stint, although he never allowed himself to become a real part of the organization. Wherever he is, there is something in Bill that seems to keep saying, I should be somewhere else. I am afraid this restiveness will be with him always.

If the old guard had passed or was passing among our on-air personalities, this was even more true of CBS News management. Salant and I were at retirement age, Bud Benjamin nearly so and Ernest Leiser past sixty. Bill Small was gone. That left only Bob Chandler, who had both experience and comparative youth on his side. (Bob was now handling what had been my old job: He was in charge of *60 Minutes*, documentaries, conventions and elections.) It was imperative that I try to put a team in place that could run CBS News down the road, a group from which top management might pick a new President someday.

My informal but intense executive search turned up two names: Ed Fouhy and John Lane. Fouhy was Washington Bureau chief, Lane a senior producer on the *CBS Evening News*. They were both fairly young, excellent newsmen but lacked management experience. We made Lane Deputy Director of News, and after a year or so I brought Fouhy to New York to run the hard-news operation. Roger Colloff came up from Washington to be my executive assistant.

When it came time to discuss my own successor, I was asked by Gene Jankowski for my recommendations. Assuming Bud Benjamin was too close to my own age, I proposed Bob Chandler as the best-qualified executive. After we had talked about Bob for a few minutes, Gene said, "Now, who else?" I brought up the names of Ed Fouhy and John Lane, particularly Fouhy, the senior of the two. "It's too bad we don't know them a little better over here," said Gene, "I guess they're terrific."

Van Sauter eventually took over as my replacement. I had known him well as he handled a variety of roles, some in news, some in other parts of the company. I had always thought of him as colorful and versatile. But he had never worked with me or for me directly over the years, so I had no real way of judging his potential as President of CBS News. And that was my initial reaction to Gene Jankowski when Gene first mentioned Sauter to me as a probable successor. As it turned out, the chemistry between Sauter and Fouhy and Lane was poor. They were "Leonard's boys" and it wasn't Leonard's place any longer. Thus NBC News gobbled up two more of our people.

There is a saying in the news business to the effect that one big story is worth a hundred little ones. It sounds self-evident, but even experienced editors sometimes fail to recognize the immensity of a really big story or, if they do, to devote enough resources to it. Big news stories present big opportunities—for news organizations and for individuals. Sadly, the big stories are often tragic ones. The London blitz made Ed Murrow's career; Dan Rather was on the spot in Dallas when Kennedy was assassinated, and his career took off. There was one very major story during my own stint as the top man at CBS News, and I wish I could say that we covered ourselves with glory, hard as we tried. This was the Iranian hostage crisis, which began with the takeover of the American Embassy in Teheran in November 1979 and continued for many months.

The situation was already quite tense in Iran in December of the previous year, but since Kappy and I were returning from a trip to Asia I decided to stop there. I was pretty well connected in Iran, albeit primarily with the Shah's regime, through his Washington ambassador, Ardeshir Zahedi. I had known our own ambassador, Bill Sullivan, over the years, and I now arranged a couple of talks with him in Teheran. Sullivan thought the chances were that the Shah would survive, but he didn't sound overly confident, and other people with whom I talked were downright pessimistic. Teheran had been the scene of numerous bombings, and it was considered an unhealthy vacation spot, though outwardly it seemed pretty much the same unpleasant city I had known from several of my earlier visits.

Through my connections with Zahedi, I managed to arrange an interview with the Shah's wife, Empress Farah Dibah. Kappy and I and Bud Benjamin and his wife, Aline, who were traveling with us, spent perhaps an hour with her in a reception room of the royal palace. She was a strikingly handsome, intelligent woman, obviously under enormous strain, doing her best to be cordial and reassuring about the future. As we spoke, she twisted a diamond ring (worth probably a few hundred thousand dollars) around her finger; I got the impression that only great self-control was keeping her from screaming instead of smiling. Later that evening, I set up a circuit to New York and reported on my interview with the Empress over the CBS Radio Network. It was the last time I ever broadcast for CBS.

The next day a reception was given in our honor by Ambassador Zahedi in his magnificent home, not far from the palace. In his absence, he had arranged from Washington for a good number of his country's ruling elite to show up—the heads of the Air Force, Army and Navy, the Secretary of the Cabinet, the Shah's political advisor—their wives, too.

It was a real nice clambake. Two or three generals and diplomats cheerily assured me over champagne that the Shah was strong, that it was only the world media that were stirring up trouble. Nevertheless, I had the distinct feeling this might be one of the last times an American journalist would be entertained on Iranian soil.

The Shah fled Iran on January 16. During the purge of sympathizers of the Shah in the months following the Khomeini takeover, Bud and I would sometimes see a news or television photo of a poor manacled wretch being led away to execution. We would compare notes, and agree sadly: Yes, it's one of the guys we met at the reception.

From the time of the Shah's abdication to the storming of the American Embassy and the taking of the American hostages, it became virtually impossible for us to get correspondents and camera people into the country to cover the Iranian story. Visas were unobtainable. Americans were the enemy. What film or tape we got trickled in from French or Japanese sources.

As the story got bigger and bigger, our news sources—not only those of CBS News but of all the networks—dried up increasingly. Everyone tried crashing cameramen or correspondents into Iran. This gambit is dangerous and usually unsuccessful, but it has been known to work. Your man gets on a plane going to the country in question and when he get to the airport of entry tries to beg or bribe his way in. Four times we tried it in Iran, and four times we failed. But ABC got a critical break: Somehow, with an old visa, one of its London correspondents, Bob Dyk, slipped in just a few days before the takeover of the American Embassy.

It gave ABC News a very real lead on a story of enormous importance. Naturally, they took full advantage of it as, throughout the hostage crisis, CBS News and NBC News tried in vain to catch up. Each weeknight at 11:30 P.M. ABC presented a special broadcast, "The Iran Crisis: America Held Hostage." There was hardly enough news coming out of Iran to warrant a broadcast night after night, but for several months the public's appetite for news about the hostages was voracious. When the crisis ended, the series continued, as it does today—it is *Nightline* with Ted Koppel, a highly intelligent, able journalist. Ted had been a fine newsman all along, but his career was made by the Iran story. Coverage of this tragic chapter in recent history really lifted ABC News to the level of the other two networks. In fact, measured by aggressiveness and pursuit, ABC News became our toughest hard-news competitor during the early 1980s.

I knew that Lyndon Johnson had not been the least bit hesitant to call Stanton with complaints about CBS News coverage, but I was aware too that the working news people had been well insulated from these occasional tirades by Stanton and Salant. The tensions between the Nixon White House and the media—especially television, and CBS News in particular—were well publicized. If there were no calls from Nixon himself, there were more than a few from his aides. Morale at CBS News remained high during the Vietnam years, when the administration's effort to discredit CBS News was at its peak, largely because there was the feeling within the organization that top management would not buckle under fire.

When it became my time to run CBS News, I recognized that in the months or years immediately ahead I might have to respond to pressure from 1600 Pennsylvania Avenue, for that seemed to go with the territory.

My baptism by fire was provided by a segment of 60 Minutes called "The Iran File," which was scheduled for airing on March 3, 1980—right in the middle of the hostage crisis. The segment, produced by Barry Lando and narrated by Mike Wallace, went into considerable detail about SAVAK, the Iranian secret police, the brutality and corruption it exhibited under the deposed Shah and its somewhat cozy relationship with U.S. intelligence agencies. Certain interviews that Wallace and Lando had sought meant that advance word of the broadcast had filtered into State Department circles. Within the Carter administration, there was apprehension almost to the point of paranoia that a major media piece which painted the Iran crisis in other than black-and-white terms might somehow undermine anti-Khomeini public resolve. Of course no one in the government had *seen* the piece, but Wallace and Lando were told that, on the basis of a single interview with a former SAVAK agent they understood was in the segment, the safety of the hostages might somehow be jeopardized.

This reasoning didn't make much sense to the 60 *Minutes* people, but they warned me that Carter's aides had the bit in their teeth. Sure enough, a call came from Lloyd Cutler, Counsel to the President, who seemed to be rather mournfully doing his duty in this case. It had not been too many months earlier that Cutler had been one of CBS's top outside lawyers, a stalwart defender of full freedoms for the broadcast press. Here he was, obviously uncomfortable in a different role.

"I think Wallace and the rest of your people may have led you down the garden path on the Iran piece," he said to me.

I had looked at the segment and thought it was excellent and valuable reporting and told Cutler so.

"Well," he murmured, "if I can't convince you, you may be hearing from someone else."

A few minutes later a call came from Jimmy Carter. I was certainly not an intimate of the President's, but our casual relationship had been pleasant. I had met him on a number of occasions, and Kappy and I had enjoyed an informal dinner upstairs in the living quarters of the White House, along with a very few other CBS News people and their wives.

"Bill, I know you talked to Lloyd Cutler," he said. "I really hate to bother you."

"That's perfectly all right, Mr. President."

"Bill, 60 *Minutes* is a very important program, and this is a very critical time in the history of this country. We think it's very important for the country that you all don't run that program, or at the very least postpone it until this hostage thing is resolved."

"I understand what you are saying, Mr. President," I said.

"I hope you'll give it every consideration."

"You can be absolutely assured that I will, Mr. President."

"Well, I very much appreciate it."

After an exchange of further pleasantries, we left it at that. When we hung up I realized how difficult it had been for Jimmy Carter to make that call, and how vulnerable it left him and an administration beleaguered by the Iran hostage problem.

We could have gone to the print press with the item that the President of the United States had tried to keep a 60 *Minutes* segment off the air. That would surely have focused an enormous amount of national attention on the broadcast. However, I dismissed the notion of that sort of exploitation as quickly as it crossed my mind. Instead, I sent for Wallace and his boss, Don Hewitt, told them I had received a call about the Iran segment and said I wanted to go over the ground again. I didn't tell them the call came from Carter, but they probably guessed it. I wanted us all to be satisfied that we had not missed something that might indeed jeopardize the possible release of the hostages. Again we came to the conclusion that the program would not.

The segment went on as scheduled. There were no repercussions whatsoever after the fact, neither from the Iranians nor from the worried Carter administration.

It would be much too simplistic to say, "Always reject a Presidential request to kill or hold a story," just as, obviously, a responsible journalistic organization would not automatically acquiesce. Each case must be treated separately. Inevitably, though, any administration in power is almost certain to invoke the national interest in attempting to stifle or delay a story, when, in fact, its own interests may be what it is really trying to protect.

Years after "The Iran File" was broadcast I ran into producer Barry Lando, who told me something I had not known at the time. His feelings about the segment had been so strong that he had secretly taped a copy in advance of air time.

"The word quickly got around that the White House was putting the heat on," he recalled. "And if CBS News had killed the segment I would have resigned and found a way to have it played on the air somehow, somewhere." Barry Lando is still a producer at CBS News.

*　　*　　*

How gratifying it would be if my few years as the head of CBS News had begun, continued and ended on one note of triumph after another. But let's see now. I'm having just a wee bit of trouble dredging up sticks long enough to reach around and pat myself continually on the back. I pushed through a West Coast edition of the *CBS Evening News*, which meant the network news in the nation's largest state was no longer three hours out of date. We also opened a modern and expanded news center in London on March 30, 1981, with Tom Wyman (then President of CBS Inc.) in attendance to greet Prime Minister Margaret Thatcher.

We were all surprised at the simplicity of security precautions for Mrs. Thatcher. An hour before she arrived a little man came around and asked if we minded if he had a look. He poked about for five or six minutes, waved to us and left. That was that. Some minutes after all the opening speeches had been made and Mrs. Thatcher had departed, word came that President Reagan had been shot. Bud Benjamin and I were in the wrong bureau at the wrong time. The troops managed beautifully without us, not surprisingly.

By that time I had forgotten all about the disappointment of Election Night 1980, which I had very much wanted to be a smashing evening for the organization. It was my last election-night broadcast, but—far more important—it was Walter Cronkite's last. As usual, Walter was in top form. But NBC News took the ultimate step and, using exit polling, called states almost as soon as the polls closed, with what seemed to be reckless abandon. Warren Mitofsky, our veteran election expert, and I were betting that at least one of their calls would turn out to be wrong, and I guess that's the way we were rooting. But they all stood up. Ironically, however, NBC won the battle that night but lost the war, reaping a bitter harvest of criticism for using exit polls well, but perhaps not too wisely.

For sheer pressure and excitement there is nothing more stimulating than holding down a key position at one of the networks on an election-night broadcast. It is the only very big story that takes meticulous advance preparation and that unfolds dramatically before one's eyes, perhaps with the fate of the world hanging on the result, if the Presidency is at stake. Getting ready for election night is not unlike training a horse for the Kentucky Derby: enormous preparation for an event in which the stakes are high and which is over very quickly. I really miss being a part of election-night broadcasts. I'll have to concentrate on winning the Derby.

When the state of the news warrants extra programming, 11:30 P.M. Eastern time is the standard slot offered to the news division. Only the most extraordinary events warrant the expense of invading precious prime-time hours, when a preemption will cost hundreds of thousands of dollars in lost revenue and very probably have some negative effect on the total audience for that evening if it comes early in the schedule. For years Dick Salant and I had lobbied for a regular informational broadcast at 11:30 P.M., without any success. From the point of view of the network, it apparently did not make economic sense. I was told whenever I pursued the subject and pointed to the success of *Nightline* that it was a guaranteed money loser. My answer was I couldn't prove or disprove that, but I wished to hell the CBS Television Network could do such a broadcast. The best I could get was a smile, and not much argument when I said I needed to preempt 11:30 P.M. for one night, which we did time after time during the period of more than one year while Iran held American hostages in captivity.

We had some successes. One was a series of broadcasts that aired for five consecutive nights in June 1981, entitled "The Defense of the United States." The debate over the proposed U.S. arms buildup was a matter of intense national interest at that time, and it seemed incumbent upon us to do something well beyond mere coverage of the controversy on our regular news broadcasts.

In planning what we would do, I felt that a one-hour "worthy" examination of the nuclear threat and American readiness in the face of that threat would be simply swamped in the theater of prime-time entertainment. The subject was too big, too important. If we were going to tackle it at all, we had to do it in a dramatic, all-out way. Why not do *five* hours in a single week? If that didn't open the eyes of the American people to the nuclear threat, nothing short of a real war was likely to.

Gene Jankowski grasped the importance of the project, which would, obviously, cost the network a good deal of money—all the profit from the scheduled reruns would be gone, plus the considerable cost of producing five special one-hour broadcasts. The total amount would be somewhere in the neighborhood of $2 million. But with surprisingly little struggle, and in a surprisingly short time, I got the green light and turned the project over to an able young team. Howard Stringer, who later went on to be producer of the *Evening News* and President of CBS News, was named executive producer. Andrew Lack was the producer.

The team had been working for a couple of months when Stringer walked into my office and gave me his tall, British smile. "Boss, I hope you don't mind, but we're planning to blow up Omaha." He paused for effect.

I did not bite.

"Nuclear, dammit. Nuclear!"

"Sounds like a barrel of laughs," I said finally.

"Seriously," said Howard, "we're going to try to show something of what a nuclear bomb would do to a city. Using models, and a lot of effects. And Omaha. It should make the point."

It did. Omaha was nuked on the first of the five broadcasts in a highly dramatic sequence that showed in the most vivid terms the devastation that a single atomic explosion would cause. All five of the broadcasts were powerful and informative, if not perhaps quite as explosive as that first one when Omaha disappeared before America's very eyes.

The CBS Network had promoted "The Defense of the United States" heavily. And because the idea of a five-part documentary on a serious subject on successive nights was so unusual, the print press had written about the broadcasts extensively in advance. The normal documentary attracts perhaps 18 percent of the available viewing audience. On its first and second nights, "The Defense of the

United States" drew nearly twice this many people, or about as many as watch a hit comedy series. The reviews that followed were full of praise, and the series later won nearly every major documentary award for that year. Even though I was quite far away from the programming end of the business most of the time I was President of CBS News, with "The Defense of the United States," and one other project, I felt as if I had done my part to improve the quality of network television.

For a number of years Dick Salant, Gordon Manning and I (later Salant, Small and I) would work up a list of projects CBS News would like to do if the time and money became available and the climate was right. A longer *Evening News* headed the list, and after that a late-night news broadcast and a longer morning news. Somewhere on the list, year after year, was a Sunday broadcast that would be offered at a time when people had some leisure and would feature a more relaxed look at the world, particularly America.

The Sunday idea got little attention. The early hours of that day especially were considered a useless ghetto into which were crammed kiddie cartoons, the remains of CBS's once splendid religious programming, presided over by Pamela Ilott, and *Face the Nation*. After that, "real" television could begin, with sports leading the way, as the nation woke up to what it was all about, and the commercials that made it all possible.

All the networks had generally abandoned the early Sunday hours to their local stations, which in recent years had found an unexpected bonanza in paid religious programs. There is no limit to the ingenuity of man in seeking the almighty dollar, and seeking the Almighty is one of the surest paths to earthly reward, particularly with the help of a television station. CBS stations by the score had given up CBS early Sunday programming in favor of shows featuring local gospel preachers who paid hard cash for this otherwise useless air time.

Still, I had a mental picture of the kind of American couple who like to spend a leisurely Sunday morning reading the papers, perhaps turning on their television set if there was anything worth watching. I couldn't get the idea of a Sunday television magazine out of my head. And even before I had officially taken over as President, I spoke to Gene Jankowski about it.

I suppose during my first few months as President of News I was the beneficiary of the kind of honeymoon that any new chief executive enjoys. I must have sounded more like a network salesman than a news executive, though.

"Gene, Sunday morning's a desert, the last remaining desert in television. If we pour water on it, we can make it grow. Believe me!" He believed me, and *Sunday Morning* was born. I had no doubt at all that the success of the series would depend on the host, and I wanted Charles Kuralt.

Kuralt, whose character is as rich and as fine as his voice, was not an easy sell. Life "On the Road" agreed with him. He was happy crafting his own pieces in his own fashion, as free as a man can be in America, with an appreciative audience when he appeared on the *CBS Evening News*. Eventually, of course, he said yes to us. Thank God, for without Kuralt *Sunday Morning* would surely have failed.

I was lucky in the choice of a producer. Robert "Shad" Northshield is almost as proud of the number of times he has been fired as of the places where he has worked. Several of his dismissal notices are framed and hung in the bathroom of his home for visitors to enjoy. (As one of his best friends once said, "Shad was born with a four-letter word in his mouth.") He had spent more time at NBC than CBS News over the years, but somehow he was a CBS News fellow of the old school, and happily he was back working for CBS when the *Sunday Morning* opportunity came along.

Shad and I met at my home in Washington one day in the early fall of 1978 and I outlined the elements I thought *Sunday Morning* should contain. "I think we would like the viewers to feel they are curling up to their Sunday television set," I began. "Let's do this program for people who say there's not a goddamned thing on television." We spent a couple of hours going over the kind of specific elements I felt should be in the broadcast, among them criticism and analysis of television itself. The program that went on the air a few months later was not far from what Shad and I outlined together that day.

Sunday Morning, like *60 Minutes* a one-hour magazine program, had several other things in common with its illustrious predecessor. It too had an energetic and imaginative producer. Without exception, the television press was enthusiastic about the broadcast, wrote extensively about it and helped introduce it to people who might otherwise not have discovered it at all. That helped a lot. And, as with *60 Minutes*, its audience grew slowly. Though of course never as popular as *60 Minutes*, and with a very much smaller audience, *Sunday Morning* is just as remarkable, especially if one remembers it is a program that is aired at 9:00 A.M. or earlier. And in its first two years on the air, its share of the Sunday morning audience increased more than 100 percent.

Sunday Morning still commands an intensely loyal following the better part of a decade after its introduction, but I am saddened to see fewer and fewer resources at its disposal. I was gratified that, by the time I retired, *Sunday Morning* was actually making money for CBS. Not much, but the desert actually did bloom a little in that unpromising time slot. I hope the time never comes when the exigencies of the television business completely bury that small acre of greenery.

It was *Sunday Morning* that gave me the notion that maybe—just maybe—I could lick the perennial *CBS Morning News* problem. There it was, near the top of that list of priorities I had talked over with Gene Jankowski in Greece months before: Improve and expand the *CBS Morning News*. Over the years, CBS News presidents stretching back to Sig Mickelson had tried just about every combination this side of Bob and Ray in their attempts to make CBS News number one with morning viewers. First there was Cronkite. Yes, Cronkite, years and years ago. Then Mike Wallace, Harry Reasoner, John Hart, Bob Schieffer, Hughes Rudd, Phyllis George, Sally Quinn, Charles Collingwood—even Will Rogers, Jr., for

God's sake. (Had we ever been first in the morning? No. Close? No. What *was* there about CBS in the morning? Make that, What *is* there about CBS in the morning? In recent years we seem to have given up trying to be *best* in the morning as well as trying to be first in the morning.)

Charles Kuralt was a marvelous host of the new *Sunday Morning*, relaxed and easy, old-shoe—but without the scuff marks. He was just folks—but never corny. He was wide-ranging—but did not come across as an egghead. The viewer mail about Kuralt that crossed our desks was extraordinary. He was well-known, of course, for his "On the Road" pieces, some of which had been worked into prime-time programs, but as a personality he had not quite registered with the impact he made on that off-hours little *Sunday Morning* program. I believed then, as I believe now, that the secret of making an impact in the morning is on-the-air personality above all else. We had had an absolutely superb hard-news broadcast in the morning for years, yet inevitably it trailed *Today*, with its long history of engaging hosts, and *Good Morning America* with David Hartman.

Perhaps Charles Kuralt could be *our* winner. Not perhaps. For certain. "You have an instinct for these things," one of my vice presidents said, his lips turning a nice shade of brown. But how was I to accomplish this? Kuralt had even balked at tying himself down with *Sunday Morning*; the idea of adding five wickedly early mornings a week to his schedule, and confinement in a New York studio, held little appeal for him. And, since he is simply not the kind of man whose eyes pop at the mention of more money, we couldn't dangle that carrot in front of him.

But we *really* wanted Charles. We wanted the Northshield-Kuralt team turned loose weekdays. Just about everyone went to work on Charlie: We need you! Here's our chance! Don't let us down!

Charles Kuralt was perhaps the youngest of the CBS News old guard. To be truly needed was like a call to arms. So finally Kuralt said yes, he would give up the life he loved, struggle out of bed gritty-eyed at three every weekday morning and follow in the footsteps of all those good men before him who had given CBS News in the morning their best shot.

To go with Kuralt we needed a woman, a coanchor—well, not *quite* a coanchor. There were two strong possibilities. One was Connie Chung, an ambitious, attractive former CBS correspondent who had gone to the West Coast and was successfully anchoring a news broadcast in Los Angeles. She came East to plead her case, radiating confidence and determination to get ahead. (She has done so, but not as Kuralt's cohost.) Connie Chung might have been a good choice, but in this case she ran second to a formidable competitor, a woman of less experience, yet with a brilliant future: Diane Sawyer.

Diane had an interesting background. She was working as a researcher for Richard Nixon after he left office, having worked earlier as a White House communications aide. In Washington, she came to the attention of Bill Small, then CBS News Washington bureau chief, who gave her a chance as a reporter in the Washington bureau when her job with Nixon wound up. It is fair to say that Diane never got a break around CBS News Washington: If there was a dirty assignment, she got it; if there was a miserable stakeout, Diane was sent. The smart money around the bureau had figured Diane wouldn't be around very long. First, they thought, look where she'd been working before she came to CBS. Second, she wasn't *really* a journalist. Third, nobody that good-looking should be in this business anyway.

But Diane Sawyer made it. And not on her looks. She made it because she worked harder and better than just about anyone else. She hustled. She dug. And it turned out she was a cool, reasonably smooth broadcaster as well. By the time the choice for the Kuralt coanchor had to be made, Diane Sawyer—by then the CBS State Department correspondent—was recognized as the most important woman in the future of CBS News. Shad Northshield insisted she was just right for the retooled morning news; Don Hewitt could hardly wait to add her to the list of hosts of 60 *Minutes;* and the CBS *Evening News* staff screamed that taking Sawyer out of the State

Department would rob the nightly broadcast of one of its most compelling assets.

The final decision was mine. I chose Diane in spite of her comparative inexperience as a daily broadcaster—indeed almost because of it. Her future was so bright, I felt, that the sooner she got daily on-the-air experience the better.

As far as I could see, our morning news program had everything going for it: a new title *(Morning)*, a revised format, even an earlier start, which gave us a better shot at competing head-on with the other networks.

Morning went on the air with considerable attendant promotion and publicity. We congratulated ourselves. We had the answer—in the CBS News tradition. Television critics, with perhaps one exception, seldom find fault with Kuralt, and Diane Sawyer seems to be just right in whatever job she is given to do. But for all of our effort, the CBS morning audience remained about the same, a respectable but definite third behind the other two networks.

In a few respects, I was not too happy with *Morning*, but this had nothing much to do with either Kuralt or Sawyer. Many of the news and feature pieces were overly long, and the broadcasts had an excessively leisurely pace. Weekdays were not Sunday mornings, after all, but sometimes one would hardly suspect it. There was something almost too comfortable about the whole effort, bordering on the self-indulgent. With the benefit of hindsight, I suspect Shad Northshield was the wrong producer. When all was said and done, *Morning* added up to just one more expensive, well-intended good try in the long history of CBS morning failures. Since that time there have been other variations on the morning theme, but none has done well.

The best thing to come out of *Morning* was a polished Diane Sawyer, just as everyone hoped, so that it was natural and fitting that she should move on to *60 Minutes*. Thus far, Diane has been a solid member of the reporting team. But whether she can go on to live up to her full potential—that remains an open question, regardless of the fact that she has joined the "million-a-year" club.

*   *   *

When I think of the amount of time I spent in the last years of my career wrestling over budgets, I have to look back in some kind of sorrow. Budget makers pay heed: In a whole lifetime of pruning, scrapping, balancing and cutting, cutting, cutting, you will not pile up a single memory. Not one. You will never run into old Al or Peter or Marie and holler "I'll *never* forget the time we trimmed $65,000 out of the London Bureau travel allowance. Remember the look on Barney's face?"

Forget it.

Programs are something else. Broadcasts, obviously, are what our business is all about, although sometimes this is forgotten.

Broadcasts are what I remember.

In autumn 1979, the campaign for the Presidency was already well under way and, not at all surprisingly, on the Democratic side attention began to focus on Senator Ted Kennedy. Without having announced his candidacy, he was an early possibility as a challenger to an unpopular president, Jimmy Carter. The old scandal of Chappaquiddick kept bubbling up, however, hand in hand with any talk of a Kennedy race. Late in September, I talked with Bud Benjamin, Howard Stringer and one or two of my other associates about the idea of a documentary centering on Kennedy and Chappaquiddick or simply an interview with Kennedy. Another Chappaquiddick investigation, so many years after the event, was not too appealing: CBS News had done a thorough one years before and there had been endless print replays over time.

I came to the conclusion that we should do a prime-time one-hour interview with Kennedy and that Roger Mudd should conduct the interview. He seemed to me to be the only correspondent with the combination of interviewing skills and political savvy who might successfully pull such a delicate interview off, for Chappaquiddick would obviously have to be one of the subjects. Mike Wallace had the skills, but I was sure Kennedy would not sit still for Wallace.

"Do you think Mudd would do it?" Bud Benjamin asked me. "You know they're good friends. The whole family."

"I think maybe he's a journalist first," I said, "and he would regard this as a perfectly legitimate assignment, which it is. If Ted Kennedy doesn't want to do the interview, he can always say no. He's a big boy."

I had honestly never expected that he would say yes, but I was delighted and mildly surprised when the word came back that Kennedy had agreed to be interviewed by Roger Mudd. The rest, as they say, is history. I cannot recall a single television interview with so devastating a negative impact on an important political candidacy. "Teddy," which aired on November 4, 1979, revealed a fumbling, inept Kennedy, simply unable to handle himself well during the broadcast.

The audience was fairly large, and the aftershock was enormous. It spelled the end of what had looked like a serious Kennedy challenge to Carter. Though sad to see this happen, I was proud of the broadcast and the job that Mudd and producers Stringer and Lack had done, proud because CBS News had made an important contribution, helping at a critical time to reveal the thought and character of a major political figure. "Teddy" was a broadcast to remember.

By spring 1981, Ted Turner's Cable News Network had become critically successful although still a money-losing proposition. Ted was making the first moves toward offering a version of his service to over-the-air broadcasters. CNN's immediate impact was still more potential than actual, however, since not enough people nation-wide tuned regularly to CNN to compete significantly with the three major evening news broadcasts. But the long-range implications of a twenty-four-hour news service available to CBS affiliates made us wonder whether we should not take steps of our own to offer viewers the same service or something close to it.

I commissioned a study of what such a service might offer, and how much it would cost. We had a very fine newsgathering organization already in place, and it seemed logical to expand it to something like a round-the-clock service. But when all the figures were in, it made no economic sense to create such a service, certainly not merely as a reaction to some vague down-the-line threat from Ted Turner.

Gene Jankowski and I talked it over.

"It looks like it might be a hell of a lot cheaper just to buy CNN," I said, half in jest.

"Do you think we could?" asked Gene.

"I don't know. Doubt it. But stranger things have happened."

A few days later I was on the phone with Bob Wussler, Turner's right-hand man and once mine.

"Bobby, what would happen if our two bosses and the two of us had a little talk?"

"That might be fun."

So began the first skirmish in the Ted Turner–CBS war. A company plane flew Jankowski and me to the private aviation airport in Atlanta. Shortly we found ourselves in a motel room nearby (this was an ultrasecret meeting), face to face with the man who had spent a good deal of time in public calling CBS programs a disgrace to America, and CBS News people "scum." Turner was wearing an open-neck sport shirt, jeans, Top-Siders with no socks—and he was apparently chewing tobacco. He kept a water tumbler on the table next to him, and by the time we had completed our chat he had filled it with a heavy brown juice.

"How are you guys?" Turner began. "How's old Paley?"

"Fine," one of us said.

So much for small talk.

"I'll sell you CNN," he said abruptly.

I waited for the other shoe to drop. Neither Gene nor I said anything.

"How much of it do you want to buy?" Turner asked.

"Fifty-one percent or more," said Gene.

"You want control? You don't buy control of Ted Turner's companies. Forty-nine percent or less."

"No, honestly, Ted," I interrupted, my heart in my mouth. "You know CBS. We just wouldn't be interested in less than fifty-one percent."

"You guys," he said, striding around the room, "you CBS guys are something. Someday I'm going to own you, you bet I am. Remember I told you so."

We all laughed.

"Sure I can't sell you something? I can't come away from here without selling you something! How about my wife? Lovely lady."

We laughed again.

The meeting was just about over. The four of us piled into a car and drove back to the airport. Turner hopped aboard the CBS plane for a quick look-see.

"Hey, some terrific plane! Wanna sell it to me? Well, what's the difference? I'll own it anyway one of these days."

Gene and I boarded the plane and flew off, and I haven't seen Ted Turner since.

But CBS has.

The most controversial, if hardly the most acclaimed, of all documentaries in CBS News history was initiated, completed and broadcast (January 23, 1982) while I was nominally still President of CBS News, although Van Sauter was chief executive officer and had been named to succeed me. Curiously, my name never surfaced during the widely publicized trial it provoked, in which General William Westmoreland sued CBS for libel. (The suit was later withdrawn.)

I recall that nearly a year earlier Mike Wallace and producer George Crile had come to me to talk about a documentary idea, which they described as very explosive. Crile said he had evidence that the U.S. command in Vietnam had "cooked the books" and deliberately reported a smaller number of enemy troops opposing our forces than they knew actually existed. Crile said he and Mike already had one incriminating interview with an officer, Sam Adams, involved with intelligence estimates at the time, and that he was certain he could get many others, including one with General Westmoreland. I was extremely doubtful, to say the least.

I had, of course, no way of knowing whether in fact enemy troop estimates had been massaged, but I could hardly believe that a group of responsible American officers, including the commander of U.S. troops in Vietnam, would get on camera and reveal this to the American public. My instinct was to tell Crile and Wallace to drop the whole idea, not because these allegations had no truth to them, but because we would probably spend a great deal of time and money and end up with something we could not pin down. But, in spite of my grave doubts, I said, "Okay, if you can get those other officers to confirm the premise of this broadcast, and if you can get Westmoreland to talk on camera about the situation at that time— then we can think about going ahead. These things either happened or they didn't happen." I never expected to hear about the subject again.

A few months later, Howard Stringer bounced into my office. "Hey, we got Westmoreland!" he shouted. The Westmoreland interview sealed the validity of the premise of the broadcast in my mind. If he had refused to be interviewed—for that matter, if Westmoreland had denied in the interview that the enemy troop count had been underreported—I never would have approved going ahead with the project.

As the broadcast neared completion, I was drawn into some discussion concerning its title. Crile very much wanted the word "conspiracy" used; he insisted it was a conspiracy and that the title should say so. I thought that was simply too strong a word. I cannot remember a documentary that caused more haggling over its title— we must have discarded twenty or thirty possibilities. I don't know how the final one—"The Uncounted Enemy: A Vietnam Deception"—was developed, but it was a compromise, and no one was particularly happy with it.

I screened the broadcast in late November and was generally very much impressed. More than anything else, I was astonished that Crile had been able to document his material so convincingly with on-camera interviews with responsible officers—the very thing I felt would be impossible when he and Wallace introduced the idea in my office months earlier. I did not probe too deeply into the broadcast, nor did I give it its final screening. Van Sauter did that, and gallantly assumed responsibility for a broadcast with which he had precious little contact, except to promote it with more flamboyance than perhaps proved wise.

George Crile was an archetype of the kind of producer whose broadcasts were almost certain to be fascinating, unconventional and highly controversial. A documentary he had produced a couple of years before "The Uncounted Enemy" dealt with the political power of the gay community in San Francisco and aroused some violent protests from viewers who felt it had been slanted against homosexuals. But Crile was always ready to defend his work, chapter and verse, and he had this opportunity in excruciating detail in testimony during the Westmoreland trial.

It is fair to say that I was always of two minds about Crile, as were many of my associates. We were impressed because he was a hard-digging, extremely hardworking investigative reporter, fully capable of using television effectively, which meant that his work moved swiftly and dramatically. On the other hand, we sensed a lack of objectivity, a quality that it is not unusual to find coupled with stubbornness. After the San Francisco documentary there were some informal discussions concerning Crile's future with CBS News, resulting in a tepid vote of confidence. I am certain that the question of his future arose again following the Westmoreland affair. For whatever reasons, he is still with CBS News, as a 60 Minutes producer, and, from what I am able to observe, doing excellent work.

Toward the end of September 1980 I had been asked to continue as President of the news division for one year past my sixty-fifth birthday, which would be in April 1981. I would be the first executive in CBS history except for William Paley himself to have the company retirement policy pushed aside in his favor. I was under no illusions concerning the company's motivation: It was simply convenient. Ahead, in spring '81, lay the departure of Walter Cronkite and the arrival of Dan Rather on the Evening News. I was closely tied to both events, and it did not make sense for a new man to step aboard in the middle of that traumatic transition. No one ever discussed this with me; Gene Jankowski simply asked me one day if I would stay on, and the next day I said I would, and that was that.

Even after having figured out what it was all about, I could not help but be pleased. It *was* a record-setter, whether I had backed into it or not. Who was it who said invitation is the sincerest form of flattery?

By the time the date approached for Walter to turn the *Evening News* over to Dan Rather, I had the feeling he was already beginning to regret that he had given up the job. Instead of looking genuinely happy at the prospect of retirement, he seemed to be keeping up a brave front, while the entire United States of America prepared to send him on his way as if he were a favorite god who, having spent a while here among the mortals, was now returning to heaven. "Jesus, I'm not *dead!*" he snorted, as the press rained farewell editorials upon him.

Consciously or not, perhaps Walter noticed during his last few weeks that while Cronkite was uppermost in the thoughts of all those good folks out there in TV land, he was not the center of attention at CBS News. Dan Rather was. For the future rested on Rather's shoulders. I had made this decision: Changing the *Evening News* anchor from Cronkite to Rather would be traumatic enough for our regular viewers; I did not want them further unsettled by noticing that the immediate environment surrounding the anchorman was appreciably different, too. Not for a while. So, with some minor adjustments (Rather's longer legs meant raising the anchor desk chair), we planned to start Rather off from what was basically the Cronkite anchor position, while working on a new set in another part of the 57th Street building.

Several of our research people across town had warned us about something any damn fool could guess—that when Cronkite left the *Evening News*, there would be a falloff in our audience. How much, and for how long: Those were the questions. Longtime

Cronkite fans would sample all three evening news broadcasts and finally settle on their choice. Obviously, the Cronkite departure offered NBC and ABC a heaven-sent opportunity to capture some of our audience. Hoping viewers would make the connection between "trusted" Walter Cronkite and John Chancellor, NBC began running on-the-air promos with the tag line "John Chancellor and the NBC News team. Experience you can trust." ABC ran at least five big print ads, plus numerous radio spots and television promos.

We were far from inactive in the war for the hearts and minds of the news viewer. Our television spots talked about CBS News's "history of excellence." Our print ads emphasized Rather's credentials for the job. And a full-page ad in major newspapers paid tribute to Walter while also emphasizing his new responsibilities and assignments at CBS News, including documentaries and the science series *Universe*.

As if his sterling record were not enough, Walter capped his last week with a one-hour exclusive interview with President Reagan from the Oval Office of the White House on March 3, 1981. I was pleased to be there, along with Bud Benjamin, who produced the broadcast, Ed Meese, James Baker and other members of the President's inner circle. As the interview drew to a close, Mr. Reagan said, "I know you must be having a little nostalgia; the many presidents that you have covered in this very room . . ."

"Indeed so, sir," Walter answered. "I was counting back. It's eight presidents. It's been a remarkable period in our history."

And then the President: "May I express my appreciation. You've always been a pro."

Those were enormous shoes to fill, and when Dan Rather took over on March 9, 1981, it was by no means certain that he could fill them—especially with 20 million or so people watching intently, perhaps with some displeasure, ready to test the new boy on the block.

Dan had been the substitute anchor for Cronkite many times, particularly since the announcement that he would succeed to the job. He had great presence, but he was not as smooth a broadcaster as Roger Mudd, or nearly as relaxed as Charles Kuralt. I don't particularly like to find myself using the word "performance" in connection with news, but there's no getting away from it: The news has to be "delivered." Dan's performance that first night was no prize-winner. We kept telling each other he was *going* to be fine, and I was sure of it. Well, almost sure. He did not seem at home. It was not quite his broadcast.

As the weeks went by, however, I thought he improved noticeably. But inexorably, perhaps inevitably, our ratings drifted downward. CBS News was no longer in its accustomed number-one spot. The public had not yet caught on that Dan had finally arrived.

When Van Sauter arrived on the scene in late November 1981, soon to replace me as President of News, he made a series of successful production changes in the *Evening News*, some of them editorial, some cosmetic and, together with Dan's steadily improving self-confidence and grasp of his role, turned the rating picture around. As I had every expectation he would, Dan rose to the occasion of special broadcasts, and I believe this helped his image a great deal. He was excellent in a crisis—when President Reagan and Pope John Paul II were shot, at the time of air disasters, conventions and elections. He is today, in fact, far and away the best in the business up there alone on a running big story. I have never regretted the decision that made Dan Rather anchorman and managing editor of the *CBS Evening News*, win, lose or draw in the ratings race down the road.

During the summer of 1981, Jim Rosenfield, Executive Vice President of the Broadcast Group, a staunch friend of CBS News, talked to me about plans he and his people had devised that he said could result in an hour-long *CBS Evening News*. "I *think* we've got it worked out so that it will be so attractive financially for the affiliates that the majority will go along. At least I hope so," he said excitedly. This was just what I had hoped would happen—the network and the news division working hand in hand to convince affiliates that a full hour of news coverage was in their best interests. Accordingly, Bud Benjamin and I worked hard to prepare an attractive presentation of what a one-hour news broadcast might contain, and this was ready, along with Rosenfield's sales pitch, when we met in November with the governing body of the affiliates, the Affiliates Board, in Hawaii. I had the unqualified support of Tom Wyman, who was also present.

The relationship between affiliates and a network is a delicate and subtle one. It varies greatly depending on the size of the station, smaller stations being generally more dependent on their network for programming—though no network can arbitrarily impose its programming during time that normally is filled locally. What we were talking about filling with our hour-long news program was probably the most precious local time, and the most profitable: the dinnertime period. An expanded evening news, while welcomed by some stations, was seen as anathema by many others, forcing them to cut back their local news service.

To make a long, complicated and sometimes acrimonious story short, the affiliates horse, led so carefully to water, refused to drink. CBS's third attempt—and probably its last—to schedule a one-hour nightly news failed, and with it one of my fondest hopes. It did not founder because the majority of affiliates questioned its potential content, or even the ability of a long network news to draw and maintain a typical news audience. It failed because the most powerful affiliates, and groups of affiliates, said in effect that it simply did not make dollar sense for them.

I was bitterly disappointed. I was certain then, as I am now, that the news warrants and the country needs a national news broadcast by one or all of the three major networks longer than the present half hour. More than a quarter of a century ago, executives at CBS and CBS News thrashed out the question of whether to extend the news from fifteen minutes to half an hour. The argument against it then was that there wasn't enough news around to fill that much time. Nowadays, however, there is apparently plenty of news in Hometown, U.S.A., especially if it includes extensive weather and sports coverage. Many local stations, some even in comparatively small cities, find ample material for an hourly news broadcast each night. And at the network level, PBS does an interesting hour, although it lacks the resources for wide-ranging on-the-spot coverage.

Once during the time I was head of CBS News, Gene Jankowski offered me what he described as a "bigger job." "I'm reorganizing the Broadcast Group," he said, displaying the same boyish enthusiasm with which he greets almost everything. "And you would come over here and be responsible for news not only at CBS News but at the owned stations, too." I asked Gene if there would be someone else running CBS News, and he said yes, there would be, but that person would report to me, and I would make more money. I told Gene I would think it over and get back to him. It crossed my mind that he might be kicking me upstairs. But upstairs was not a place to which I had the slightest desire to go. I was already on the highest landing that a person in the television news trade could hope to reach. The corridors of Black Rock were jammed with presidents and vice presidents, and most of them made more money than I did anyway. But there was only one President of CBS News. Men and women had risked their lives, and some had given their lives, for CBS News. In fire and flood, in World War II, in Korea, in the civil rights struggle and in Vietnam. CBS News was a palpable thing, something to be proud of often, perhaps to be ashamed of occasionally, to be defended always—but not to be promoted from.

I called Gene up and told him I wanted to stay exactly where I was. And so I did.

By the beginning of 1982 Van Gordon Sauter had taken over the reins of the CBS News Division, and on February 28 a number of CBS people, some of whom I had worked with for more than half of my life, gathered in Studio 41 to say good-bye to me. Studio 41 is the big CBS studio, the one in which I had planned and we had broadcast so many elections. It was home plate. Many kind things were said, and the walls were decorated with blowups of old pictures that proved I had once been young. Or at least younger. I hated like hell to leave, but I knew it was time to go.

But in truth I have never left, not in my mind or in my heart.

13

FINALE

During the period of turmoil at CBS News in 1986, a newspaper reporter, casting among the battered former presidents of the place for some quotable morsel, asked me what there was about CBS News that had made it so special. "After all," he said, laughing, "it's not *The New York Times*."

"No," I said, "but we always wished we were."

Unhappily, though, since 1982 I had been watching CBS News trade away its aspirations and its high standards for quick fixes. I could understand that the pressure was mounting inexorably on those who had succeeded me—the pressure, above all, to be first in the evening news race. The pressure, too, to show progress in the morning. To some degree, nothing had changed over the many years since Mickelson, Salant, Friendly, Salant again and then I had stood between the news division and the looming bottom line. All of us had known what that was all about. The pressure came from the top; it was inherent in the system. The ratings performance of the *CBS Evening News* was a simple way to keep score. And whenever trouble got big enough there, the response was just like baseball: Try a new manager. Fair enough.

But for all the ups and downs, all the small and large triumphs and the raging controversies, that elusive quality called morale—a treasure for little teams and great nations alike—never seemed to flag at CBS News until strife within the division and within the company cut it to shreds in very recent years.

Somehow, I can't help feeling that this very palpable loss of morale crept up on CBS people as a result of the attitudes of management: The top management appeared to have come to regard CBS News as almost more trouble than it was worth, and the management of the news division itself began to think of it as just a step on the corporate ladder.

How different it had been once! I never heard the word "duty" in the boardroom or the cutting room in all my years at CBS News, but an unquestionable sense of duty was what kept the division so remarkably united. Men like Bill Paley and Frank Stanton had a sense that their duty extended beyond their stockholders, beyond their employees to viewers and listeners. Their conscience dictated that they had a duty to inform as well as entertain. A cynic might say theirs was the virtuousness of a Sunday churchgoer, but, as a close observer of both men over many years, I do not believe that was the case.

A CBS News person of my time would have snickered at the idea that "duty" had anything to do with what made his or her relationship with the place special. Duty? West Point stuff. But in truth a rather extraordinary sense of obligation did run through the place, as if the privilege of being there—stamping one forever—should be paid back with extra effort. The spirit of Ed Murrow and his fierce independence haunted the halls. There was the sense that at least this part of the company was marching to a drummer other than the laugh meter, and that William S. Paley knew it, understood it and approved of it. As Bill Moyers said, "Do you come to work to escape the day or engage the day? CBS News believed the latter."

There is new-old management at CBS now, with a stated strong commitment to CBS News, and CBS News now has a vigorous young leader, Howard Stringer, whom I have known for nearly twenty years, almost since the day he first set foot in the West 57th Street building that houses the news division. He is gifted and articulate, utterly different in personality from Friendly and Salant; he is a more easygoing and engaging character, although perhaps in his own fashion no less committed to the institution.

It remains to be seen, of course, whether CBS News has left most of its recent internal turmoils behind. I suspect not. I am even inclined to say I *hope* not. For we should remember that, except for the fuss and feathers about the departure of Van Gordon Sauter and Ed Joyce before him, whenever CBS News became page-one copy in the past, principles or programs were usually involved: Murrow vs. McCarthy. "Harvest of Shame." "Hunger in America." "The Selling of the Pentagon." The General Westmoreland documentary. If today's CBS News is living up to its past, there are surely unknown challenges in its future, and they are certain to test the courage of the men and women of the news division and the company as a whole.

I suppose the question I am asked most often is whether I believe there is any real future in network news. I do believe so. The networks—joined in recent years by CNN—fill a genuine public purpose with their news broadcasts. As a cohesive nation, we would be at a loss without them. In the year 2000, some ask, what would the television industry have to offer? The answer is simple: network news. There will be network news as long as there are networks. And the competition among networks will go on.

In a very real sense, the network news broadcasts are all that distinguishes one network from another. Entertainment shows come and go; they are interchangeable from one network to another—indeed, sometimes they actually shift from one to another. The network news, and the network news capability in times of emergency, is what gives a network its individuality, year in and year out.

One day I read that technology will put us out of business, that local stations can do anything networks can, and do it cheaper and better. The next day I am told "choice" will ruin us, that by the year 2000 every television set will have 1,456 competing channels. And the day after that I read that it is a "bottom line" philosophy that is squeezing the networks to death, that in order to survive they must, among other things, cut back their news divisions. Of these three threats, the last is the most serious. Yet it has been around for a long time; the squeeze has always been on to one degree or another. It certainly was no stranger to me in my years at CBS. People who are not in the news business find it hard to understand that in news, as in everything else in life, there is a tendency to get just about what you pay for. Good news coverage is assured by hiring good people, and good people are expensive. Adequate coverage of fast-breaking stories requires speed, and speed is expensive. Good documentary work often requires patience, and patience is expensive. A very real danger for the year 2000 is not that we will have less network news but that we will have poorer-quality network news.

What the president of a network news division mainly does is fight for money and time on the air. That is what we did at CBS in 1960, 1970 and 1980. That is what Howard Stringer is doing in 1987 and what someone will be doing in the year 2000.

I wish each of them luck and spine.

INDEX

234